CHINA TAKES OFF

CHINA TAKES OFF

Technology Transfer and Modernization

E. E. BAUER

Introduction by Michel Oksenberg

University of Washington Press   *Seattle & London*

Copyright © 1986 by Eugene E. Bauer
Printed in the United States of America

All rights reserved. No part of this publication may be reproduced or transmitted in any form or by any means, electronic or mechanical, including photocopy, recording, or any information storage or retrieval system, without permission in writing from the publisher.

Library of Congress Cataloging-in-Publication Data
Bauer, E. E.
  China takes off.
    1. Technology transfer—China. 2. China—Economic conditions—1976–   I. Title
  HC430.T4B38 1986   338.951'06   85-17984
  ISBN 0-295-96298-4

Jacket photo: At the hinge of two worlds, an invisible "technology curtain" separates the ancient from the modern. All photos by Eugene Bauer unless otherwise noted.

To Beth
for helpful suggestions
and constant encouragement

INTRODUCTION

by Michel Oksenberg

For somewhat over a century, Americans have been on the China mainland in significant number: missionaries, businessmen, journalists, foreign service officers, soldiers, doctors, scientists, engineers, students, and so on. Americans began residing on the China coast even earlier, first restricted under the confining conditions the Chinese traditionally imposed upon foreigners, and then exploiting the opportunities and privileges for foreigners under the Treaty Party system.

In the later part of the 1800s, the numbers began to grow, and in the first half of the twentieth century, Americans lived all over China. They concentrated in the coastal enclaves in Shanghai, Nanjing, Beijing, Tianjin, and Guangzhou, but Standard Oil employees found themselves in such remote areas as Wan Xian in Sichuan province. Ethnographer Joseph Rock studied national minorities along the Yunnan-Burmese border. Oberlin University developed its program outside of Taiyuan in tradition-bound Shanxi province. Yale sponsored its medical program in Changsha, Hunan province. American engineers surveyed prospective hydroelectric projects on the Yangtze and Yellow Rivers. While their total number remained low, Americans were spread throughout the country. Then came World War II and the influx of Chennault's airmen, Stillwell's ground forces, and numerous United States government officials from the Office of Strategic Services (OSS), Office of

War Information (OWI), Treasury, and so on, all intended to assist our Nationalist ally.

All this ended rather abruptly in 1949–50, with the communist revolution, the Korean War, and the campaigns against the Western presence in China. A few Americans languished in Chinese prisons until 1955. A few others secured employment with the new government as translators, economic advisors, teachers, doctors, and social workers. These were joined by a handful of American prisoners-of-war who chose to remain with their Chinese captors rather than return home.

From 1950 to 1971, in short, less than fifty Americans resided on the Chinese mainland. But Americans continued to have intimate contact with Chinese in Hong Kong and Taiwan. With President Nixon's overture to the People's Republic in 1971 and even more with the Chinese opening to the outside world following Mao Zedong's death in 1976, Americans once again began to live on the mainland. Old ties were restored. Yale went back to Changsha, Oberlin to Shanxi.

Some things were different. No American military advisory groups or expeditionary forces undertook work on the mainland. No missionaries began to preach their doctrine, though similarly motivated successors began to teach English throughout China. The pattern of interaction is different, too, for both Americans and Chinese have changed in the interim. Our country is perhaps somewhat less self-confident, less imbued with a sense of mission. China has galvanized itself, is unified, less vulnerable to exploitation. A greater degree of equality and reciprocity attends Sino-American relations today than in the past.

To date, the histories of Sino-American relations before 1949 have tended to concentrate on the political dimensions and on diplomatic history. Beyond that, the missionary movement in China and cultural and intellectual exchanges have received primary attention. The commercial and scientific dimension has been relatively neglected. Sherman Cochrane's study of the British-American Tobacco Company and Mary Brown Bullock's account of the Rockefeller Foundation–funded Peking Union Medical College are exceptions.

One reason for this neglect is that Western businessmen and technicians in China rarely recorded their experiences through memoirs, diaries, and personal archives. For this reason, future scholars as well as current students of China will long be thankful for this book by E. E. Bauer.

It is a fascinating and insightful account to today's China from a unique vantage: that of a Boeing engineer assisting his colleagues at the Civil Aviation Administration of China (CAAC) to learn how to maintain B-707's and B-747's. In a very real sense, Bauer was at the cutting edge of the Sino-American relationship from 1980 to 1984. Few industries and products embody the complexity and sophistication which the airline industry and aircraft contain. China's turn to the outside world has included the commitment to transform CAAC from a small and sleepy company into a modern, international airline. Modernization of its fleet and operations are, of course, the key. With the purchase of ten 707's in 1973 and three 747's in 1979, Boeing has been centrally involved in this process.

In short, technology transfer to China is not a new phenomenon. It has been going on for over a century. But Bauer is among the few to make vivid how such a transfer actually occurs: the difficulties, the frustrations, the cultural differences, the intrusion of politics into the process, and also the satisfaction of participating in a historical process. He is an astute observer, and the book is full of penetrating insight into the Chinese condition.

Two big questions exist about today's China: Will the opening to the outside world persist, and will China's drive for modernization prove successful? On both counts, Bauer is a cautious optimist. This is not unusual, but he provides a unique perspective for his argument. His book reveals the Chinese thirst for foreign technology and equipment. Indeed, using the aviation industry to illustrate his point, he shows that they cannot modernize without it. As to the chances for success, Bauer believes that it will not happen immediately or swiftly. But during his four years there, his Chinese colleagues began to change age-old approaches to technological issues. Bauer witnessed their growth and capacity to learn. Extrapolating from the experience with the 707's and 747's, there do not appear to be insurmountable cultural obstacles to China's growth.

Here, then, is a book for the present and the future, for businessmen and journalists seeking insight into present-day China and for historians decades hence who will study the process of technology transfer to China in the 1980s.

ACKNOWLEDGMENTS

Sincere thanks are extended to *China Daily,* which served as a valuable source for statistical data, as well as for pertinent quotes from leaders of government, agriculture, education, and industry. Reprinted by special permission.

Grateful acknowledgment is given for use of short quotes from a number of publications.

"A China Daily in America." Copyright © 1983 by *Newsweek* Inc. All rights reserved. Reprinted by permission.

"A Storm Over China's Airline." Copyright © 1983 by *Newsweek* Inc. All rights reserved. Reprinted by permission.

"China Intensifies Campaign To Attract More Tourists," by Frank Ching. Reprinted by permission of *Asian Wall Street Journal,* © Dow Jones & Company Inc., 1982. All rights reserved.

"China Stinks," by James Kenneson. Copyright © 1982 by *Harper's* Magazine. All rights reserved. Reprinted from the April 1982 issue by special permission.

"China's High 'Friendship' Prices for Foreigners," by Scott D. Seligman. Reprinted by permission of *Asian Wall Street Journal,* © Dow Jones & Company Inc., 1982. All rights reserved.

"China's Political Course: Causes and Prospects," by Michel Oksenberg and Richard Bush. Reprinted by permission of *Asian Wall Street Journal,* © Dow Jones & Company Inc., 1982. All rights reserved.

"End of an Era for China's Farm Communes." Copyright © 1983, *U.S. News and World Report*. All rights reserved. Reprinted by permission.

"For China, Another Great Leap Nowhere," by Sol W. Sanders. Copyright © 1983, *Business Week*. All rights reserved. Reprinted by permission.

Myself a Mandarin, Memoirs of a Special Magistrate, by Austin Coates. Copyright © 1968, Heinemann Asia. All rights reserved. Reprinted by special permission.

"Population Lid," by Amanda Bennett. Copyright © 1983, *Wall Street Journal*. All rights reserved. Reprinted by permission.

"Where Mao Danced, Capitalists Now Deal," by Frank Ching. Reprinted by permission of *Asian Wall Street Journal*, © Dow Jones & Company Inc., 1982. All rights reserved.

"Why China Has Opened Special Economic Zones," by Ji Chongwei. Copyright © 1984, China Reconstructs. All rights reserved. Reprinted by special permission.

"Why Tourists Pay More." Copyright © 1982, *South China Morning Post*. All rights reserved. Reprinted by permission.

PREFACE

"Tian gao huangdi yuan."—old Chinese saying

"THE SKY IS HIGH and the Emperor is far away." The origin of this saying is buried in history. But if one were to choose from a countless number—there is one for every situation—it would closely portray the centuries-old Chinese attitude. In the 20th century Deng Xiaoping, China's new strongman, boldly declaring a sweeping modernization program, revived an old slogan, originally made in the aftermath of the Great Leap Forward in the 1960s. "It does not matter whether a cat is black or white, just so it catches mice" became the new watchword.

Many in the West anticipated an overnight inpouring of Western goods and Western methods. However, it was soon clear that there could be no "great leap" from antiquity to a modern society. The educational base was too shallow, infrastructure in the vast nation was woefully lacking, energy resources were only beginning to be tapped, and the intellectual and cultural fabric of China's massive population had been dealt a ravaging blow by the ten-year Cultural Revolution, a purgatory that did not end until the passing of Chairman Mao in 1976.

In January 1980 I went to China to establish an office for Boeing. As part of China's new modernization effort, the purpose was to aid in the integration of jet airplanes into the fleet of the Civil Aviation Administration of China (CAAC), which had embarked on a serious program of international competition. In 1973, as a result of the historic Nixon/Chou En-lai (Zhou En-lai) meeting of 1972, the CAAC initiated a significant growth phase, taking delivery of ten new Boeing 707 jet airplanes. Then, in February 1980, the first 747 jumbos touched down in Beijing.

Orders for Boeing 737 and McDonnell Douglas MD-80 Series airplanes followed, and in April 1985 a contract to cooperatively manufacture MD-82 airplanes in Shanghai was signed. Indeed, 1985 brought a dramatic acceleration in the modernization of China's commercial airplane fleet. Purchases were also announced for the British BAC 146, the Russian TU-154, the Airbus A310, and the Boeing 767.

At the time of my arrival, the CAAC was emerging from the dark ages of airline operations. Food on the planes was so bad that foreigners simply refused to eat it. In China, where people must obtain permission to fly, the airlines felt it sufficient to sell a seat, even considering this a favor. On many domestic flights, the atmosphere was enlivened when a stewardess would invite the passengers to join in singing revolutionary songs. The CAAC had developed such a bad reputation that the official Chinese newspaper, the *People's Daily*, began a systematic attack on its management. Almost immediately, with great fanfare, the CAAC launched a "quality service month," calling on all employees to provide "civilized service." However, as in most campaigns, the passing of a month signaled the time to fall back into many of the old habits.

I use the airline as an example of the change and growth throughout China that began in 1979. Traditionally, aircraft manufacturing is regarded as the flower of industry, and a successful international airline carries the message of progress and outreach to the world. Thus, the airline and aircraft manufacturing represented a microcosm of all industry in China, indeed the bow wave of its industrial modernization.

Sloganeering is an important ingredient of everyday life at all levels of society in China, resulting in temporary bursts of enterprise and enforced enthusiasm. In a country of edicts and directives, the masses have never known the need for innovative undertaking. The most important—and constitutionally guaranteed—part of the Chinese day was the two-hour *xuixi* (nap).[1]

Everywhere the Chinese attitude impeded progress. Workers did not seek initiative. It was far better to be submerged in the masses and do what was bidden. Then whatever went wrong could not be blamed on the individual—and did not beget punishment. As a result of this history and attitude, it was all too easy for contemporary writers on China to become preoccupied with the excesses of Chairman Mao, the Cultural Revolution, the Gang of Four, and all that was bad in the country.

China will not evolve into a highly technological society within the next several decades. Perhaps it will take a century; however, there is good reason and ample evidence to believe that the change can be accomplished during the next three generations. So far, advances in technology, even though spectacular on some fronts, represent only the thinnest of veneers, overlaid on a peasant society.

Nevertheless, not enough has been said about the new direction that China has taken since 1979. The sweeping goal of quadrupling the gross national output by the year 2000 appears to be unduly ambitious. However, the boldness of the vision of the new leaders, and their singleness of purpose, force the world to take note. Simply stated, China is a developing country, determined to improve the economic status of its 1 billion people. With a confidence and courage seldom seen in a world leader, Deng Xiaoping has pressed forward, drawing followers with fresh ideas around him.

[1] Article 43, Constitution of People's Republic of China, December 4, 1982. The two-hour nap came under official attack in 1985.

The object of this book is to present a perspective of the new China as perceived from day-to-day events in a struggle to introduce an infrastructure, where there was none before; to instill a desire to work, where there was only a reluctant response to orders; to learn the Western language of engineering and computers, where there were only pictures and sounds; to communicate, where communication was often dangerous; and, above all, to develop a feeling of individual worth in a nation where, prior to 1979, eight-tenths of the people toiled with a single purpose—to provide food and shelter for the coming winter.

CHINA TAKES OFF

CHAPTER 1

LEAVING SEATTLE in the bright sunshine of a beautiful and unusual January day was difficult. Having lived in New York City, immersed in the overpowering noise, pollution, crime, and traffic for a full year, we found that Seattle had offered a brief breath of hope and welcome relief. We watched this all fade into the contrails of the Northwest Airlines 747 that lifted us into the cloudless sky, heading northwest along the Washington coastline, seeking the thread of the 53rd parallel.

With me on this new adventure was my wife, Beth. We had just wrestled seventeen bags and boxes through the SeaTac terminal, containing our carefully selected support items to begin our stay in the People's Republic of China. My mission was to establish an office for the Boeing Commercial Airplane Company in order to aid in the integration of modern jet airplanes into the fleet of the Civil Aviation Administration of China.

It was 1980, scarcely fourteen months after President Jimmy Carter, in his historic meeting with Deng Xiaoping, brought about the normalization of relations with the People's Republic of China. The China of 1978 that Carter and Deng had addressed was attempting a 180-degree turn, away from antiquity and isolation and toward Western technology and cooperation. My mission represented a part of that effort. In less than thirty days, a new 747 airplane was scheduled to touch down at the Beijing airport and join the CAAC fleet.

Approaching Beijing from the air at night in the dead of winter, we had not expected much, but nevertheless craned our necks to see a bit of the city. There were no signs of the great metropolis of 9 million people. The flare of light that surrounds our Western cities was missing. Only an occasional, pencil-thin beam stabbed the darkness. Soon, two or three of the main streets were vaguely outlined by rows of pale lights, the entire scene masked by a translucent film. There seemed to be no city at all!

During the base leg to the airfield, the runway lights came brilliantly into view, and we could see the terminal building of the new airport, completed a scant two months before. A single row of lights speared a path into the heart of the city. In the darkness, the surroundings were indistinct. However, a finger of a modern jetway soon appeared, and we quickly passed through the "technology curtain" into the People's Republic of China. And so began a period of five years of strange experiences, unusual sights, terrible frustrations, difficult living conditions, and severe environmental surroundings. However, the Chinese proved to be gracious hosts, helpful, considerate, and willing to provide the best they had from their poorly developed country.

A chill blast of wintry air greeted us as we walked into the jetway and started the long march to the customs and baggage area. Upon arrival, two large U-shaped moving belts appeared immediately in front of us. Several smiling Chinese stepped forward with outstretched hands to greet us. They were officials of the CAAC who would be making arrangements for our stay. The spokesman, Mr. Xu Zhengle, Director of Outside Purchasing for their Headquarters Offices, was a gracious host, fluent in English and determined to make everything as comfortable as possible. The Chinese smiled a lot—I found later even in difficult situations. For me, they proved Abraham Lincoln's famous observation that a person is about as happy as he makes up his mind to be.

We had expected cold weather in Beijing, but were unprepared for the sub-freezing temperature inside the terminal. Small clouds of vapor rose from each silent figure as we waited in the dimly lighted interior. Bundled in their padded cotton uniforms, with three or four layers of clothing underneath, the Chinese were oblivious to the cold. In an all-saving society, there was no logic in heating the massive terminal building during the night.

After an interminable delay, the belt began to chug forward, coughing luggage out of its dark maw. Finally, after forty-five minutes, I spotted the first familiar bag, and soon we were ready to depart. In the parking lot, cars and mini-buses were standing helter-skelter, devoid of pattern or organization. Lighting was poor, people were milling and shouting, but we finally crammed the mass of luggage and all the people into the mini-bus for the ride into the city.

Outside, the landscape was dark, and, from what we could see, it was bare and lifeless. Austere, forbidding, chilling, colorless—these words tumbled through my mind as we drove down an arrow-straight two-lane roadway between rows of freshly planted trees. We were pleased to note that driving was on the right.

Although the main road was reasonably well lighted, the darkness was total only a few yards on either side. In Beijing, as in most of the country, electricity was scarce, and full lighting was seldom turned on. Also, driving with headlights was forbidden, a concession to the army of cyclists who swarmed the streets. Drivers kept flashing their lights for brief moments to see their way and as a warning.

It was nearing midnight, and the cold became more harsh and brittle as a stiff wind riffled whorls of dust on the bare ground on either side of the roadway. It was our baptism by the Beijing winds— and our first introduction to the dust.

Conversation in the mini-bus was sparse. Of the Chinese, only Mr. Xu Zhengle and the interpreter spoke English, and, aside from pleasantries, we were immersed in our private thoughts.

Horse-, mule-, and donkey-drawn carts began to appear, the twin spikes of vapor expelled from the animals' nostrils an eerie sight under the dim street lights. The drivers were bundled in padded uniforms, the flaps of their huge fur caps waving in the wind as they snapped their whips, urging the laboring beasts onward. We thought it strange that most of the carts were loaded with dirt, but we learned that one of the main activities of the Chinese peasants is to move dirt and rock. Occasionally, a cart with a battered steel drum or a rusty rectangular tank came clanking past, carrying the famous "night soil" or human fertilizer out to the fields.

Soon apartment houses appeared. Rows of rectangular, eight- and nine-story buildings in various stages of construction illustrated the campaign to change Beijing into a vertical city to avoid further encroachment on the precious farmland by the expanding population. In 1980, the year we arrived, 32 people occupied the same space as one person in the early 1930s.

After 30 kilometers of the same cold, gray, dreary landscape, we arrived at the center of the city and the famous Peking Hotel. A goal of all foreigners coming to the capital was to obtain lodging there, specifically in the newest addition, the 580-room east wing completed in 1974. All other hotels in Beijing, in fact in all of China, were considered to be primitive by comparison.

The central city was buried under a pall of smoke. We were actually within two blocks of the hotel before we saw it, a 17-story building, highest in the city. Tragically polluted by extensive use of high-sulfur coal, Beijing's air had been tested by U.S. Environmental Protection Agency representatives and found to be six times higher than the safe breathing level. During the winter dust precipitates amounted to 39 tons per month per square kilometer. We were informed that breathing the air during the heating season was equivalent to smoking two packs of cigarettes a day!

At the hotel, we were assigned a room on the third floor of the east wing. A single room! Expecting a two-room suite, we hid our disappointment and were told that it was a victory merely to be admitted into the east wing. Business people already established in suites were being urged to find locations elsewhere, as the hotel's preference began to swing toward tourists. I was disappointed to learn that the rumor of an antibusiness climate was true. In spite of the "modernization" slogans, businessmen were given the lowest ratings of any class in accommodations and support. Capitalists were welcome only if they brought plenty of money—and spent it freely.

The China that greeted us that bitter winter of 1980 was already very different from the People's Republic that Chairman Mao had proclaimed on October 1, 1949. At the time, he was not only Chairman of the Communist Party, but of the new Republic itself. Nine years later, in 1958, Chairman Mao initiated the "Great Leap Forward," hoping for an overnight industrialization of China. He had not reckoned with his vast, unwilling homeland and its threadbare infrastructure. By 1965, the skeletons from the hundreds of thousands of backyard iron-smelting furnaces were stark monuments to the dismal failure of the Great Leap Forward.

Indeed, Mao had been replaced as Chairman of the Republic by Liu Shaoqi. Worse, he had been openly criticized by the Politburo. With grievous political wounds, he returned to

Shanghai to form a new strategy and to regroup his forces. He viewed the maneuver as would a battlefield commander—taking a small retreat while he prepared for his next great victory.

Scarcely six months had elapsed when Mao launched the "Great Proletarian Revolution," a last-ditch attempt to recover the idealism, drive, and religious fervor with which the early revolutionaries maintained their thrust on the Long March. The magic of his name attracted hundreds of thousands of young and eager hands to his cause: unofficial armies of "Red Guards" who denounced everyone whom Mao chose, and many more. Liu Shaoqi was disgraced and died soon thereafter.

China was caught in a gigantic convulsion. The power-drunk Red Guards rampaged out of control through the cities. Anarchy and civil war threatened. Intellectuals were the most bitter targets. Teachers were sent to the countryside for reprogramming and cleansing through work in the fields. Schools were closed and books burned. Those who worshipped Buddha quietly and tearfully buried the symbols of their devotion to avoid censure.

In the decade that followed, China lost the education of nearly an entire generation—the very generation that it so sorely needed to carry the burden of the new modernization programs. The failure of Mao was papered over by the accusation and trial of the "Gang of Four," but eventually officials admitted that Mao himself had made "serious mistakes" in the implementation of otherwise "perfect principles." By the time of Mao's death in 1976, the country was exhausted. With constant revolution and endless turmoil, people had begun to cry out against the futility of their lives.

Mao's hand-picked successor, Hua Guofeng, had nothing new to offer, and as a strict revolutionary he continued to point to the "capitalistic elements" as the regime's worst enemies. Indeed, Deng Xiaoping, to whom the greatest role was to be given in the modernization campaign of the late 1970s, had been labeled as the "number two capitalist roader"[1] in the Chinese leadership hierarchy and had come under open fire in 1966.

Himself a survivor of the Long March with Mao, and a tenacious fighter as commander of the 2nd Field Army, Deng was present at the ceremony marking the founding of the People's Republic held in Beijing on October 1, 1949. After his fall in the mid-1960s, Deng returned to grace in 1973, only again to be stripped of all his positions in the Party and the Government in April 1976, when he came under attack by the Gank of Four.

After the exposure of the Gang of Four, Deng bounced back, and by 1977 was being proclaimed by some as a superstar, regaining all the posts he had relinquished. The dedicated search for new beginnings by Deng led to the normalization in December 1978. By the time Beth and I reached China somewhat over a year later, the major immediate objective of Deng's policies—improvement in the standard of living—was already being felt.

Without realizing it, we found ourselves at the hinge of history in China, at the eye of the hurricane, its calm belying the currents of change that surged around us. Mao's engine of revolution had long since spent its spontaneity, and the masses were willing to embrace any new policy that promised them more freedoms and better lives.

Nevertheless, Deng, and the followers whom he was gathering around him, had inherited a two-legged colossus, with one foot still firmly entrenched in the hard leftist incantations, the other feeling its way in a quicksand of yet-to-be-firmed ideology. It is only necessary to observe the efforts in creating a constitution, to realize the herculean task that Deng had taken

---

[1] *Teng Hsiao Ping, A Political Biography,* by Chi Hsin. Cosmos Books Ltd., 1978.

upon himself as merely a Vice-Chairman of the Party and a single member among many of the Standing Committee of the Politburo.

We were witnessing the transformation to a rigid governmental system that could replace the one-man rule of Mao and still cope with the administration of the needs of 1 billion people. In order to come to grips with the multifaceted problems left in the wake of the Revolution, Deng and his associates promoted collective rule, while retaining the system of absolute control over all the aspects of society.

The four modernizations—modernization of agriculture, industry, science, and defense—were proclaimed in that order of priority, with completion targeted for the year 2000.

The problems that Mao bequeathed to his successors have been succinctly summarized by Oksenberg and Bush:[2]

> Lagging agricultural production
> An inefficient industrial system
> High unemployment among youth
> A low standard of living
> Widespread apathy and cynicism
> An inadequate scientific and technological manpower base
> Specific bottlenecks in transportation, communication, and energy
> An unacceptably high rate of population increase

As China's new management embarked on the unexplored ocean of hoped-for modernization within this century, one of the most pressing requirements was hard currency to purchase the sorely needed products of Western technology, a goal perceived to be the only way quickly to close the technological gap. It was not difficult to pinpoint the areas of the economy

---

[2] "China's Political Course: Causes and Prospects," *Asian Wall Street Journal*, February 24, 1983.

that were capable of providing hard currency: selling raw materials to the West and drawing tourists into the country who would bring fistfuls of cash. Early emphasis was placed on tourism and the development of mineral resources, particularly petroleum, which by expert analysis were potentially huge, notably in the extensive continental shelf surrounding southeastern China. Tourism was only a word on paper in 1977. Hotels were scarce and inadequate. Transportation facilities into China by air were very limited. Within the vast country itself, railroads were the principal mode of transport. In mountainous southwest China, where many of the important tourist attractions are located, there was not a single trunkline prior to 1949, only a narrow-gauge railway in Yunnan Province.

The automobile was never a major form of transportation in China; hence a national highway system is nonexistent. With the production level of 220,000 motor vehicles in 1980, consisting primarily of trucks and utility vehicles such as jeeps, the passenger car is rare. Airplanes lend themselves admirably to bypassing the need for an expensive road-building program, while being able to open remote areas to tourism and commerce. Thus, the Chinese emphasized hotel building and improved transport as two of the highest priority projects.

Like many of its industries, China's Civil Aviation Administration was entering an era of dramatic change. In order to meet the mandate of the national will in expanding tourism, they needed a complete overhaul from top to bottom. Their fleet was old, consisting largely of Russian-built airplanes. In fact, the airline, established in 1952, was a Chinese-Soviet undertaking. Known as SKOGA, its purpose was to take over and expand air services in China, which until then had been provided by the Central Air Transport Corporation (founded in 1931 with German capital as the Eurasia Aviation Corporation) and by the China National Aviation Corporation (CNAC).

The new airline began its services with Lisunov LI-2s,

(Russian-built DC-3s) between Beijing and Hangzhou, Kunming and Canton, and to Chita, Irkutsk, and Alma Ata to link up with Aeroflot's services to and from Moscow. The title, Civil Aviation Administration of China, was adopted in 1954 when Russia's 50 percent holding reverted to the Chinese government. Domestic and regional services were gradually developed, but it was not until 1973 that the CAAC made its first long-haul flight, following the arrival of the five Russian IL-62, four-engine jet transports. In August of the same year the first delivery of the Boeing 707s took place, and by the end of May 1974 all ten of the airplanes had been delivered to Beijing.

In those days, all procurement was handled via the Ministries. Machimpex, the machine-building arm under the Ministry of Foreign Trade, had responsibility for buying airplanes, engines, and parts. However, the winds of change were moving rapidly, and in February 1980 the government vested the procurement of airplanes and associated equipment in the CAAC and, subsequently, an internal branch, the China Aviation Supply Corporation (CASC), was formed.

When I arrived, the 164 airplane CAAC fleet, in addition to the ten 707s, consisted of 36 British Tridents and 6 Viscounts, with Russian planes making up the remainder. At that time, six domestic airlines in the United States each possessed more planes than the entire CAAC fleet. The first big task for the CAAC was to absorb and implement the three new 747 aircraft that Machimpex had purchased in 1979. It was a bold undertaking. The 747 represented the most sophisticated commercial aviation technology that the world had ever produced.

CHAPTER 2

THE CHINESE were solicitous and concerned that we would need considerable rest after the long trip, and insisted that we spend the morning in our room. The afternoon, they said, would be soon enough for me to go to the office. Their custom was to take a *xuixi* every day after lunch, and they were surpirsed that foreigners did not follow the same practice.

The *xuixi* grew out of the ancient peasant custom of rising with the sun and working in the fields until dark. The break was taken at midday. Since the People's Republic was proclaimed in 1949, *xuixi* had become one of the most important and endeared rituals of Chinese society, lasting two hours in the winter and two to three hours in the summer. Now institutionalized, it has been included in the consitution.

I quickly found that nothing was allowed to interfere with *xuixi*. When 11:30 approached, even during intense discussions, the Chinese began to glance nervously at their watches. Then at precisely 11:30 they announced that it was time for lunch and simply got up and left. There was another practical reason for promptness—the first to arrive at the dining hall was likely to get the better and larger servings—and, if a minute past the posted lunch hour, nothing.

I discovered that the Chinese badly needed their naps to help compensate for their protein-poor diet. They live almost exclusively on rice and vegetables. According to Butterfield[1], Western studies showed that food consumption per capita in the late 1970s was actually only about what it was in the mid-1950s and, more surprisingly, no better than in the 1930s. These studies suggest that the average daily calorie supply in China was between 2,000 and 2,100 per person, compared to the United States level of 3,240. The average Chinese consumes only 26 pounds of meat a year, which includes 12 pounds of fish.

My new interpreter, Mr. Yu, a young, fresh-faced man in his mid-twenties, kept advising me to "Take a short rest." After learning a few Chinese words, I had a ready response, *"Xuixi wu fenzhong,"* or "Take a five-minute break," which was always good for a laugh.

I was fortunate to have Mr. Yu in those difficult early months of supporting the airline, but it was not until much later that I fully appreciated him. It was standard practice to rotate interpreters regularly, to avoid establishing friendships, or having too much of Western culture wear off on them. Suspicious of foreigners, and each other, the Chinese had a policy of maintaining insecure relationships. Once a week they were required to spend several hours in political and ideological orientation.

My first trip back to the airport, where the Boeing office was located, was a revelation in daylight. Viewed at the street level, the thoroughfares were filled with wave after wave of bicycles—a sea of wheels and spokes. In a city of 8 to 9 million people, there were 3.2 million bicycles in 1980, 90 percent of which were on the streets sometime during the day, many traveling the breadth of the city both morning and evening. The CAAC had agreed to provide daily transportation, and I was afforded the elegant service of being chauffeured to

---

[1] *China—Alive in the Bitter Sea*, by Fox Butterfield. Times Books, 1982.

my airport office each morning and returned to the hotel each evening.

In a practiced cadence, the bicyclists pedaled along, maintaining a set stance on their machines, warding off the cold with many layers of clothing. Some wore white masks tied tightly over their faces, with only their eyes showing, to blunt the wind and filter out the dust.

Production of bicycles has been one of the bellwethers of the modernization progress in China, with annual production increasing from 8.5 million units in 1978 to 27.6 million in 1983. With a total of 158 million bicycles operating in China at the end of 1983, one bicycle was available for 6.4 people, compared to one for each 16 persons in 1978.

Other than Changanjie, the celebrated central street that widens to 16 lanes at Tiananmen Square, there were few thoroughfares in Beijing. However, several were under construction, and by the end of 1981 a perimeter road had been completed around one-half of the city. There were only four overpasses in Beijing, but seven more were in the planning stages.

Travel was badly constricted by the ancient Chinese courtyard system, a collection of walled-off enclaves, each several hectares in area, separated by alley-wide streets usually choked with bicycles and miscellaneous hybrid vehicles, including horse carts. Although forbidden in the central city during the day, horse-drawn carts made many deliveries during the night. Sweepers, cleaning up the manure in the mornings on Changanjie in front of the Forbidden City, were a common sight.

In a city determined to convert from an industrialized area to a government and cultural center, new factories for heavy industry were not allowed, and a forest of vertically stacked cranes attested to the intense campaign to replace the old brick, stone, and mud residences with apartment houses.

In winter, all the people, men and women alike, wore identical clothing—loose-fitting green or blue, padded, two-piece uniforms, sandals, and *mao* caps. On colder days, the men wore fur caps with long earflaps; the women depended on scarves or luxuriant masses of black hair to keep their heads warm. Either sex might wear heavy olive-drab overcoats. Beneath the loose outer garments were three to five layers of underclothing. These garments essentially stayed in place throughout the winter, officially November 15 to March 15. The rule was to acclimatize by "putting on layers slowly in the fall and slowly removing them in the spring." By the summer of 1981 there was a noticeable trend away from the rigid Mao-inspired dress, with varying styles and even bright colors beginning to appear.

The trip to the airport was depressing. On every side the drab gray buildings, in various stages of disrepair, attested to universal poverty. Bare ground, packed as hard as stone, greeted us on every hand. I learned that Chairman Mao had ordered all the grass to be uprooted because it harbored insects and vermin. Peasant women could be seen sweeping the broad expanses of bare earth around the apartment houses and collecting horse manure from the streets.

I immediately noticed the lack of birds in the trees and the sky. "Mr. Yu," I questioned, "where are the birds? I don't see a single one."

He looked at me with a startled expression, as if I should already know. "Oh," he laughed, "they were shot."

"Shot? What on earth for?"

"Chairman Mao proclaimed them to be pests. I think they ate too much grain." Mr. Yu looked embarrassed and quickly added, "But the practice has been forbidden. It is against the law to kill birds now."

I was pleased to hear of this change. In fact, by April 1983 the Beijing municipal government announced the beginning of the first annual "Love the Birds Week." There was even a drive to build "artificial nests" for them in the woods.

Nor were there any dogs or cats to be seen. Non-productive, food-consuming animals found no place in the new Chinese society. The only exception was a occasional dog to help with the flocks of sheep. However, in South China, dogs were raised as a source of food, their meat served in restaurants.

All was in suspended animation at the Boeing office—and covered with a thick layer of abrasive yellow dust. Originally established in 1973, when the CAAC began receiving delivery of the first of the 707 airplanes, the office had been closed since 1975, when the equipment and records were moved to the regional office in Tokyo.

True to Chinese protocol, our first meeting began with the serving of tea. In the front room of the two-room suite, converted to office space in the old airport hotel, was a large conference table. Actually, four smaller square tables covered with a large white cloth, the conference table gave the appearance of immensity. The significance of that minor item was lost on me at the time, but I discovered that it represented one of the important aspects of Chinese imagery: everything must be grandiose and, if not physically so, it must be altered. *Facades are fundamental.*

Soon after Mr. Yu and I arrived, the CAAC officials came in, smiling and offering their hands in greeting. Then they proceeded to line up behind their row of teacups on one side of the table, and I took my place facing them—five cups against one! My anxiety quickened. The Chinese simply poured boiling water from the ever-present thermos bottles into the cups, which have individual covers, allowing the tea to steep as it cooled to a drinkable temperature. The huge cups served as magnificent hand-warmers in winter.

The water everywhere in China was too polluted to drink

without being boiled, so every office, factory, hotel, and private dwelling had a way to boil water. Some facilities, such as the Beijing Hotel, are equipped to boil water under pressure, superheating it with steam, with the result that the thermos bottles keep it very hot for an entire day. I expect there are more thermos bottles in China than Chinese. For drinking, the boiled water is cooled and stored in a second set of thermos bottles. Thus, we had the *kaishiu,* or boiled water, and the *liang kaishui,* or cooled boiled water. In the hotels, each floor was served separately, with a central desk to handle the daily dispensation of water to the rooms.

Each day, the city of Beijing discharged 1.9 million tons of waste water, introducing pollution into the city's underground water resources. The hardness of the water has continually increased, as well as the concentration of such harmful chemicals as nitrates, cyanide, benzene, phenol, and such heavy metals as mercury, chromium, and cobalt. Water pollution continues to be a serious problem throughout China.

At our first meeting all the principals were present, including Mr. Yu. Mr. Xu Zhengle was the leader. Tall for a Chinese, he was affable and relaxed, fluent in English, well traveled to the U.S. and Europe. Mr. Yang Bin, Deputy Director of Engineering and Maintenance, in his early sixties, was a workhorse with over forty years in the airline, dating back to the CNAC days. White-haired and crew-cut, he was a most pleasant man, with a wrinkled face wreathed in a perpetual smile. Mr. Yang had high-blood pressure and a poor heart, but, in spite of the doctor's warnings, he was a chain smoker. Past the normal retirement age, he was kept on by the airline, because there was no younger replacement.

Mr. Hu Yizhou, Director of the Beijing Maintenance Base, youngish appearing at perhaps fifty, had devoted his career to its service. An extremely dedicated man, Mr. Hu was one of the first to recognize the need for modernization of the airline.

Correctly sensing that knowledge of English would be a key requirement, he was immersed in learning the language himself. He impressed me as a man on the move.

Finally, there was Mr. Jiang Shiying, Deputy Director of the Beijing Maintenance Base, a short, gray-haired man with a sharp face and quick eyes, who chain-smoked and spoke in rapid nasal bursts between puffs.

In an atmosphere of studied tension, pleasantries were exchanged, prior to getting into substantive issues. After five minutes of incidental conversation, par for many formal meetings, we reviewed the technical questions that had been gathering for the previous six weeks, the visit frequency of our Tokyo representative, at length coming to working hours and schedules.

Mr. Xu was the spokesman. "Mr. Bauer," he began quite formally, "it will not be necessary for you to come to the office every day. You can stay in the hotel, and we will call if there is a problem."

I would have been stunned, except that I had been forewarned of such a proposal by our original representative, who had been trapped into that mode of operation in 1973. He sat in the hotel for days on end, chafing and fuming, with no regular calls, occasionally getting an urgent request. Thus he never really had an opportunity to find out what was going on in the airline. I perceived that was precisely what the Chinese were driving at. Mr. Xu looked expectant.

"I'm sorry, Mr. Xu, but that would not work very well," I replied. "If I am confined to the hotel, I might as well be back in the United States. No, I must have regular office hours."

My hosts indicated surprise, obviously expecting me to jump at the chance to stay downtown. Their preconceived notion of Americans was of a people addicted to leisure. However, I sensed that they did not take my declaration in an adversary way.

I had learned a few Chinese words and phrases during our Berlitz exposure in Seattle, and Beth and I had been practicing on our way to China. I knew that *"meiyou wenti"* meant "no problem," and that the words graded up to *"xiao"* for "small" and *"da"* for "large" problems.

"I must know about the *xiao wentis* before they become *da wentis,"* I enunciated as carefully as I knew how.

Everyone laughed. Mr. Jiang blew a huge cloud of blue smoke, as his eyes snapped merrily.

"Your Chinese is very good," Mr. Xu exclaimed, smiling broadly. Everyone added their nods.

I smiled, flattered at the reaction. "I only know a few words, but I expect to learn many more."

"That's good, that's good," responded Mr. Xu.

"I think Mr. Bauer has a good idea," volunteered Mr. Yu, who had been very supportive from the beginning.

The Chinese discussed the proposal briefly among themselves, and then decided that it was a "good idea." Mr. Xu gave his stamp of approval, and thus my first *wenti* was solved with scarcely a ruffled feeling.

That incident proved to be the first of many where I politely declined to accept a Chinese suggestion. Over the months, I found the tactic to be extremely successful, providing benefits to both sides.

Deciding to press my luck, I found the Chinese visibly reluctant when I suggested the next step. I proposed being present on the flight line for the arrivals and departures of the 747 airplanes, boarding the planes, reading the logs, and generally becoming conversant with the crews and the maintenance personnel.

There was a long silence, while the delegation glanced uneasily from one to the other. Heretofore, the flight line had been tightly closed to foreigners, the portals guarded by poker-faced, rifle-bearing Chinese soldiers with fixed bayonets. No passes had been issued. Occasional visits were limited to special cases, arranged by one of the senior members of the engineering staff. My suggestion was anathema to their mode of operation—and to their way of thinking. However, to their credit, they did not turn me down flat, perhaps recognizing that modernization would bring the inevitable pains of change.

"That way I can tell if the airplane is getting sick—and we can avoid major illnesses," I explained.

The Chinese laughed. "Yes, like a doctor," they observed.

I had scored a point, but no commitment was made for the issuance of passes. A private meeting would be required, perhaps at several levels and across several organizations, to discuss all the ramifications of my proposed method of operation.

Mr. Jiang announced the hours. "Because of the cold weather, we will work from 8:30 to 4:00 from Mondays through Fridays. Then, in the spring, we can increase the work day from 8:00 to 4:30."

And so it was. Those hours and workday schedules are essentially still in effect, except that, as more airplanes joined the fleet, I found myself working a six-day week and sometimes on Sundays. We also standardized the work day from 8:30 to 4:30, in both winter and summer. Of course, I was on call twenty-four hours a day, seven days a week, the usual policy for Boeing people in the field, but that option was rarely exercised. The normal Chinese work week was six days. Sunday was not a religious day in this society, but it was the major off-day.

To make certain of our agreement, I wrote it all down in an official letter to the airline management. The Chinese preferred written agreements and, once signed, generally honored them. The people respected authority, with obedience a prime virtue.

We had reached a turning point, and I was determined to break down the old, shielded, secret methods of operation. I aimed to have the CAAC work closely with me, learn to trust me, and to solve problems on a mutually supportive basis.

The next day, February 1, 1980, the bitter cold continued at minus 3 degrees Fahrenheit, and a stiff 30-knot wind persisted. To save fuel costs, the Chinese had barely cracked the valves on the radiators in the office, and then soldered them in place. Thus, the temperature in the office stabilized at 56 degrees F. I kept my parka, climbing boots, and wool socks on all day.

Support facilities at the airport were at a bare minimum. In fact, there was no hangar to house the 747 airplanes for maintenance operations, and all the work would have to be done in the wind, cold, and dust of the flight line.

My first task was to review available ground handling equipment and to determine the state of preparation for the 747 arrival. I was dismayed at the antiquated equipment and the state of disrepair of the maintenance shops. I marveled that the Chinese were able to operate an airline at all.

Organized into six regions to cover the 3.7-million-square-mile country, most of the CAAC airplanes were based and maintained in the Beijing region. Heavy maintenance on the airframes and engines was contracted to Hong Kong and Japan.

After being escorted to a number of shops, my spirits falling by the minute, we discovered a first-class tow truck—made in Japan. "It belongs to Japan Airlines," Mr. Jiang volunteered, smiling as if he had received a hero's medal. "But we can use it."

Suddenly I felt a little better. "That will be just fine," I said, hurrying back to the relative comfort of the car, out of the biting wind.

The next day, Saturday, Beth and I took a trip to the Friendship Store. Every major city in China had a Friendship Store, established solely for use by foreigners. The local Chinese were screened out at the entrance. Here one could purchase whatever was available in the country, which was meager when we arrived, but improved with time. Ordinary items like hand soap, toilet paper, and toothpaste were hard to find, and common items in the U.S., such as Kleenex and chewing gum, were unavailable. We looked for magazines and newspapers—Western editions. None were available. The official news agency, Xinhua, published a 5-by-8-inch mimeographed news summary each day in English. It had two parts, foreign and domestic—our total coverage. A year later we were able to purchase *Time, Newsweek, The International Herald Tribune,* and the *Asian Wall Street Journal,* as little as four days late.

Having been limited to bring 600 pounds from home, we had no radio. The television set in our room was single channel, Chinese programming.

When we departed from the U.S., we had positive plans for learning to speak Chinese. Toward that goal, we had acquired a set of instruction manuals, complete with tapes, from Dover Publications on Long Island, New York. Then during our thirty-day layover in Seattle on the way to China, we took several sessions of Berlitz—total immersion. Reaching China, we had high hopes. I quickly learned to order breakfast, exchange greetings, and employ other simple phrases. We practiced every day.

One day, not long after, when I tried out my newly minted, so far marvelously effective, Chinese in ordering breakfast, the waiter, new to the hotel, only stared. I could hear myself saying the words—so perfectly. Why didn't he understand?

On the way to the office, I discussed the problem with my interpreter. "Mr. Yu, I ordered breakfast this morning the same as I have been doing for a month, and the waiter, who was new, didn't understand a word."

"He was probably from Shanghai."

"What's that got to do with it?"

"The Han language is only universal in its written form. There are five dialects."

Further discussion revealed that the attempt to standardize on the Mandarin Han, the northern dialect, was only partially successful.

Chinese is not a language of words, but of pictures (symbols) and sounds. The history and origin of words bear heavily on usage and meaning. The literal translation of one of my interpreter's name, Ming Yilin, was "Shining Light in a Dark Forest." One day, when I asked to verify the name of the director of the CAAC's Shanghai Region, there was confusion because the called party thought we wanted to purchase some peaches. The literal translation of Yuan Taoyuan, the director's name, is "Peach Garden."

The attempt to modernize and standardize on Mandarin Han includes a phonetic alphabet, *pinyin*. However, the sounds in normal speech are enunciated differently in different sections of the country, rendering the five main dialects mutually unintelligible. In the tonal language, the tones must be pronounced perfectly; otherwise, the meaning will be entirely different. For example, in a three-syllable word, the four tones have a potential of 40 different tonal sequences, resulting in as many meanings.

Further, under the new phonetic alphabet of the Mandarin Han, Chinese geography seemed to be transformed overnight, as well as many of the common names of the people. Kuangchou became Guangzhou; Langchou, Lanzhou; Kansu, Ganzu; etc. The old standard Chinese name of Chang became Zhang; Hsu became Xu. Even Teng Hsiaoping was now Deng Xiaoping. These are only examples. Thus I found it necessary to relearn the map and the proper way to address Chinese friends when using the written word.

If there was a single element that lay at the core of the difficulty toward technological advancement for the Chinese, it was language. Only a handful could speak English, and 90 percent of those had a poor appreciation of technical terminology. Tragically, many of the technically trained people spent a decade learning Russian, which became essentially useless. A shortage of teachers, magnified by the Cultural Revolution, bode ill for a quick solution.

When considering the Chinese ability to assimilate Western technology, I tried to look at the optimistic side. My first reaction had been that assimilation would take a full century. Then I reduced my calculation to several decades, and still later raised it again. In addition to the language problem, there was a heritage of the ancient class structure, which had left the modern Chinese with a weak spirit of entrepreneurship. The security of food, shelter, and family was all-encompassing.

Further, the generation of the Cultural Revolution, which should then have been prepared to shoulder the main burdens of a changing society, had either returned to school or was back in the countryside, leaving the task to the older generation.

Retirements were indefinitely postponed. Mr. Yang Bin was a prime example of the many veterans who were being kept on at the CAAC, and he was typical of all the technology-oriented endeavors. At this writing, the total complement of highly technically trained people in China represents only a very thin veneer.

The following Sunday, we were surprised to find that there was a Christian service near the hotel. Two in fact—one Protestant and one Catholic. We attended the Protestant Church, asking our taxi driver to *deng yi deng,* or "wait a while." In Beijing, as in all Chinese cities, taxis did not cruise, so it was impossible to find one away from their home bases at the hotels. With few phones in the stores, and none on the sidewalks, the simple chore of calling a taxi became a major undertaking. The church building was only five blocks from the Beijing Hotel, so we soon gave up the luxury of the cab and walked.

The congregation was old—Christians of long standing, testing their leaders for repercussions from attending.

At the time of the Communist takeover, people were advised to bury their Buddhas and burn the prayer books. Most complied. When the constitution was revised in 1978, religion was given new breathing room. Although not actually encouraged, its existence was recognized in Article 46: "Citizens enjoy freedom to believe in religion and freedom not to believe in religion and to propagate atheism."[2] At that stage, the devil was still ahead, but there was hope.

Then, in 1982, a further step toward liberalizing the official position on religion was taken in the latest revision of the constitution, when Article 36 of the completely rewritten document simply stated: "Citizens of the People's Republic of China enjoy freedom of religious belief."[3] The article goes on to forbid discrimination of individuals by the State for believing or not believing in religion, provides for State protection of religious activities, and forbids individuals to use religion to disrupt public order, impair the health of citizens, or interfere with the educational system of the State.

We found our new Chinese-Christian friends to be a happy and amiable group. Our common ground was achieved through

---

[2] The Constitution of the People's Republic of China, March 5, 1978.
[3] *Ibid,* December 4, 1982.

the music, with everyone singing the same tunes, while using their own language.

We were not long in China, when we were introduced to the banquet routine. The initiation rite is the authentic Peking Duck dinner, which is built around the duck itself, leaving out any other meat dishes. Every part of the duck is utilized. The skin from the feet is pickled and served with the cold dishes as an entree. The liver and gizzard are fried. A type of sausage is created from the duck's blood, and a rather pleasant moldy-tasting soup is made from the bones. The meat is cut into pieces manageable with chopsticks, and folded into tortilla-like pancakes with plum sauce and green onion pieces. The delicacy is the head, split down the middle, baked, and served—center side up.

Roast duck is far from being a recent or local delicacy. It has a firm place in history, originating in the Tang Dynasty in Ch'ang-an (now Xian), more than 1,200 years ago. During the reign of Wu Zetian (695–705), the first woman to take the title of Emperor, there were two dukes, the brothers Zhang Yizhi and Zhang Changzong who were both epicures. One of their discoveries was how to roast ducks alive. An iron cage was made especially for the purpose, and placed over the charcoal fire. The live ducks were entrapped inside. Feeling scorched and thirsty, they would drink from a copper bowl filled with a mixture of vinegar, honey, ginger and salt until they expired.

Thus, the rich flavor was preserved, and the meat stayed tender, crisp, and fresh.[4]

Peking Duck, however, is relatively modern, dating back about 600 years to the Ming Dynasty.[5] The duck, a specially

---

[4] *China Daily,* May 14, 1983.
[5] *Beijing, China's Ancient and Modern Capital,* by Liu Junwen, 1982, page 232.

bred and fatted variety, is ready when it is sixty-five days old and weighs two kilograms. After the duck is killed, plucked, and cleaned, compressed air is injected between the skin and the flesh to produce a plump, firm-looking bird. The skin is then scalded with boiling water, so that the pores contract and the albumin in the skin congeals. The air under the skin expands, inflating it and producing a glossy and shiny surface. The next step is to coat the surface with syrup, which gives the duck a rich red color and makes the skin crisp when it is roasted. After being hung in a cool, shady, well-ventilated place to dry, the duck is ready to cook.

First, a precise amount of boiling water is poured in through the rump and the opening is plugged. When the duck is put into the oven, the water is converted into steam, cooking the meat from the inside, while the skin is browned. In this way, the skin becomes crisp while the flesh remains tender.

Although Peking Duck dinners are the most famous, with eight large restaurants in Beijing alone serving the meal, there are many variations in the Chinese banquet cuisine. Nevertheless, they all follow a precise ritual. Always scheduled after 6:00 p.m., but never later than 6:30, they are orchestrated to end at exactly 8:00.

The meal begins with cold entrees, and the first toast is offered by the host immediately thereafter. Usually offered with *mao tai,* a fiery, colorless liquor made from sorghum, the toast is one of welcome and friendship. The word "friendship" has become the most overworked word in the Chinese banquet vocabulary.

Next, the chief guest, seated to the immediate right of the host, is expected to respond. Meanwhile, everyone stops eating and listens, the toasts ending in the traditional suggestion for *ganbei,* or "down the hatch." For the Chinese, *ganbei* is deadly serious, more a demand than an invitation.

Then the heavy eating begins. A Chinese banquet must have

at least ten courses. I attended one in Chengdu with seventeen. The Chinese feel that if all the food is eaten, they have been poor hosts; therefore, much more food is offered than can possibly be consumed. Many banquets include soups; pork, beef, chicken, duck, and fish dishes; boiled cabbage, beans, mushrooms, bean sprouts, cauliflower, spinach, and other vegetables.

After the principals complete their toasts, the remainder of the banquet is open season for anyone to pop up with a toast, followed by *"ganbei."*

As the price per capita is increased, the exotic nature of the food escalates. There are bear paw, sharkfin, sea cucumber, birds-nest soup and pigeon eggs, all prepared in artistic and colorful ways. Interspersed are a parade of pastry dishes. Almond tea, or some other special dessert, makes up the penultimate course, with fresh fruits forming the final flourish.

In recent times, Peking Duck has been transformed from a delicacy, enjoyed by a few, to a staple dish. To meet rising demand, more and more duck farms have sprung up. However, the three-month period from egg to market was considered excessive, so the Chinese devised a method for force-feeding the ducks, reducing the period to its present sixty-five days, a practical measure in view of the massive need for food in China.

Chinese banquets were far more than mere dinners, more even than significant social events—indeed, they formed the venue for serious business discussions. Eventually I learned that one of the most important skills to be acquired in conducting business in China was to be able to direct the tone and intensity of the conversation at a banquet.

CHAPTER 3

BRIMMING WITH PRIDE and confidence, Boeing Vice-President of Sales and Marketing, Mr. Clancy Wilde, posed a standard question to Captain Qu Yanshao, Director of CAAC's Flight Operations, at a Boeing luncheon in January 1980, while I was still in Seattle: "Captain Qu, how are the 707 airplanes that we sold to you back in 1972 working out?"

Captain Qu had a fair command of English. However, like many people dealing with an unfamiliar language, he deferred to his interpreter. It was also a convenient ploy to allow him more time to think. After a brief dialogue, the interpreter replied: "Captain Qu wants to tell you that the airplanes are working quite well, Mr. Wilde, except that we have a very serious hydraulic problem."

"Oh, I'm very surprised," Clancy answered smoothly, raising his gaze, "and highly concerned that we aren't doing something. Can you tell me more about the problem?"

There followed an excited conversation between the Captain and his interpreter. "Captain Qu says the main problem is the Abex pumps, but there are other difficulties too. There have been some flights canceled and quite a number of delays."

Suddenly Clancy was all ears. Terrible news! Not at all like the praise he was accustomed to having heaped on the 707 airplanes, and a miserable start for a secure relationship with the Chinese. "Captain Qu," he announced in stentorian tones, "you can be assured that Boeing will help you in every way possible to solve the hydraulic problem."

Seated at the adjoining table, back-to-back with the Captain, I could almost feel the heat in Clancy's words. The conversation continued for an uncomfortably long time before someone broke in with more pleasant news. This was precisely the kind of trouble that fell on the shoulders of Boeing men in the field. So began a series of traumatic experiences that became loosely grouped under a general malaise called the "hydraulic problem."

When I departed for China a few weeks later, I was advised in the strongest language to get to the bottom of the 707 hydraulic problem, and quickly. Thus, it was the first technical subject that I broached in the Boeing office in Beijing.

The directive proved to be a blessing in disguise, for that more than any other single item helped me get into the guts of the CAAC's operations at the Beijing maintenance base. In the process I discovered many of the age-old practices of the Chinese, their attitudes about cost, materials, and work ethic.

To my dismay, I found that the CAAC was operating on a petty cash basis, and, further, that this practice represented a deep-seated philosophy throughout China—a legacy from centuries of shared poverty. On all fronts, this philosophy proved to be one of the greatest deterrents to speeding up modernization. The all-saving society, where even scraps of newspaper were culled out of the garbage for reclamation, did not accept the idea of discarding anything remotely reusable.

The imposition of "aircraft quality" as a standard for flying equipment did not easily mesh with such a work ethic. In commercial aircraft, with the primary emphasis on safety, materials with the slightest defect are rejected, and manufacturing processes are kept under strict control.

Early in the history of the CAAC, Premier Zhou Enlai had

set the standard for airline operation with his admonition: "Ensure safety first, improve service, and strive for flight reliability." However, the single-minded pursuit of saving pennies quite often worked at cross-purposes with providing flight reliability. Most of the mechanics were of peasant origin, and had patched their technical training on top of an inherited bailing-wire-and-rope philosophy.

One of the most dramatic and frustrating examples of the penny-saving approach was the cleaning of non-reusable filter cartridges from the hydraulic system—this, in spite of the fact that "non-reusable" was steel-stamped on both ends of the filter element. The mechanics would wash the filters in gasoline—itself a very questionable practice—proudly show me how sparkling-clean they were, and then proceed to re-install them in the airplane. Honestly feeling that they had found a way to save money, they did not appreciate the importance of the filter as insurance against damage to the high-value components. Costing approximately $30 each, the filters were intended to be removed and discarded at predetermined intervals.

With an oil pressure in the hydraulic system of 3,000 psi, tiny metal particles are forced deep in the fabric of the filter membranes, hidden from view and not cleanable. After additional pressure cycles, the particles are driven entirely through the filter wall and out the other side—back into the oil stream—disaster for the finely honed, close-tolerance mechanical pumps, which had a unit cost of $8,000 or more. It took me over a year, while several pumps were lost, to convince the Chinese that they must discard filters once the system had become contaminated with metal particles. An added burden to both profits and image was the delay or cancellation of revenue flights.

Still another hazardous and costly practice was the use of locally produced materials. In order to save money, the mechanics would substitute Chinese-manufactured oils, greases, gaskets, and O-rings that might look the same as their United States counterparts, but quite often were not equivalent and had not been qualified by test programs. The early Chinese gaskets lacked the required swelling properties, the oils lacked corrosion inhibitors, and the greases often had the wrong viscosity.

The gritty dust of the Beijing environment made it nearly impossible to do a proper overhaul on precision assemblies without a "clean room," a facility which was nearly unknown in China, probably found only in their scientific research laboratories.

Lessons learned by Boeing from the experiences of dozens of operators in many environments have led to continuing improvements in aircraft materials and systems. These refinements are traditionally incorporated in the assembly line, and offered to the operators of existing airplanes via field kits. An example was the high-pressure hoses in the hydraulic system. Made from butyl rubber in the original design, the best material available at the time, the hoses required careful quality control because of the natural tendency of rubber to become brittle on aging. Replacement frequency was controlled by a cure date stamped on the hose assembly. A new, refined design, using teflon tubing encased in a stainless steel, woven wire mesh sleeve, eliminated the butyl material, thus providing hose assemblies with extremely long life and very high reliability.

In 1973, on the worldwide fleets of 707 airplanes, Boeing offered kits to replace all the butyl hoses with teflon, recommending that outdated spares be scrapped. As a result of the entrenched petty cash syndrome, the CAAC had not yet begun a replacement program when I arrived seven years later. They simply would not spend the money—and throw away "brand new" spare assemblies, even though the "shelf life" had long since expired.

Part of the difficulty had its roots in the original procurement of the 707 airplanes. In a purely political decision, Zhou Enlai had ordered the Chinese to purchase ten 707 airplanes, with no regard for actual fleet utilization planning. Further, the crack-in-the-door of U.S.-China relations was still viewed as tentative, and the Chinese decided to take full advantage of the new possibilities of procuring technically advanced equipment. Thus, not only did the ten-airplane figure become cast in concrete, but Machimpex also felt the necessity to order an extravagantly excessive spares inventory. As an example, they purchased 40 spare engines, a 100 percent replacement backup. This spares procurement philosophy extended to all components, and included an unnecessary number of butyl hoses, most of which aged their lives away on the shelf.

It was inevitable, then, during the visit of Boeing officials a few weeks after I arrived, that the hydraulic problem should come to the forefront, even becoming a favorite banquet topic. The Chinese hoped for substantive support, perhaps in the form of receiving new hoses free of charge, in exchange for the potential of additional airplane sales.

In subsequent discussions, the Chinese were never reluctant to point out that they were poorer than anyone else, and thus it was necessary to give them a better deal. In the following days, weeks, and months, each visit of a VIP from Boeing would elicit a new entreaty for a quick solution.

However, the hydraulic problem was not easily solved. After conducting an initial, detailed review of the history of the fleet, I determined that many interrelated factors had combined to cause a steady reduction in performance. Seeking a focus for their frustration, which had gradually turned to wrath, the Chinese had zeroed in on the hydraulic pumps. With a penchant for simplified categorizing, they quickly lumped all the ills of the system into what they called the "Abex pump problem."

When the facts were all gathered, it became clear that the Chinese practices of using inferior materials for gaskets, O-rings, and seals; the continued use of over-aged butyl hoses; poor inspection practices; re-use of contaminated filters; and, above all, the gritty dust that permeated the overhaul shops, were the major factors.

Eventually, we brought Dick Moreland, technical director of engineering services from the Abex Corporation, and Harold Hillstrom, senior hydraulic engineer from Boeing, to China to help resolve the issue.

The result was a classic discussion. The Chinese simply dumped the problem on the table, still hoping for a miraculous solution. "How many of the service bulletins on the hydraulic pumps have you incorporated?" Dick Moreland inquired. "None," replied the spokesman for the Chinese engineering staff. "We couldn't see spending any more money on the pumps, with no assurance that they would improve."

When we inquired about the use of locally manufactured gasket materials, we were informed that they looked and felt the same as the approved materials. We probed for two days, finally submitting twenty-four specific recommendations for improvement. The Chinese were skeptical. Gradually, however, they invoked the recommendations, most of which were standard practices for other operators—reluctantly accepting the premise that more than petty cash would be necessary to maintain the airplanes at a reliable standard of performance.

The meetings were so intense, and the pressure so great, that the day after Dick Moreland departed from Beijing, he was hospitalized in Tokyo with a heart attack.

Nevertheless, it was eighteen months before the last of the butyl hoses disappeared from the inventory. As a result of the combined improvements, dividends were immediately evident. Airplane performance was no longer compromised by premature and frequent failures in the hydraulic system.

By the second week of February, the bare outlines of operating in China were beginning to form, and the outlook improved from dismal to plain gray. Even the weather showed a few halting signs of improvement. The Chinese celebrate the Lunar New Year, also known as the "Spring Festival," during the first part of February. It is an apt title, since by that time the wearying weather of December and January has broken the spirit and there is a longing for spring. The office temperature struggled up to 61 degrees F.

The first mail from the U.S. arrived during the second week, establishing a pattern of ten to fourteen days, but an occasional letter slipped into the surface mailbag, dooming it to a two-month trip, one-way. Cables also started coming. The price for cables was abortive, one yuan per word, in those days equivalent to about sixty-five cents U.S. I found I could send messages out by telex at one-seventh of the cost of cables by taking the two-kilometer trip from the Beijing Hotel to the Central Telephone Building. There, I queued up to punch my tapes on ancient Chinese teletype machines, took the tapes to another queue to wait for the number to be called, then rushed to a booth to send the messages—a series of traumatic tasks designed to tax the nerves of the most iron-willed.

In those days, Chinese telex attendants had the same lethargic attitude as the waiters in the dining rooms and the clerks in the Friendship Stores. Paid a standard salary, whether or not they sold anything, and unfireable as beneficiaries of the "Iron Rice Bowl," they resented the intrusion by customers into their day-dreaming and their endless chatter with compatriots. The telex operator was elated when the line was occupied on the other end.

However, incoming messages were still limited to cables, so in mid-February I launched a campaign for a telex machine in the office, a task which offered frightful odds against success. Then, on the 15th of July 1980, as I sat down to a new, modern, Extel machine and punched my first message directly to Boeing in the United States, I felt like a combination of Alexander Graham Bell and Samuel B. Morse, rolled into one. After five months of meetings, letters, negotiations, and patient insistence, mostly against a dedicated attitude that it "couldn't be done," a secure line had been installed from the downtown telephone building, and a machine lease had been arranged. With the capability to both send and receive via satellite, I felt that at least a part of my operation in China had penetrated into the 20th century. The new service resulted in a net saving of $85,000 a year.

Shortly after, Beth and I received good news when our 682 pounds of personal goods arrived. I had battled with Boeing while still at the JFK airport in New York in 1979. When asked how much personal goods we needed in China, I drew up a carefully considered list, totaling 1,740 pounds. Boeing said "too much"—emphatically no! After excruciatingly re-evaluating, I reduced our luggage to 800 pounds. Boeing suggested 300. We settled for 600, and packing added 82 pounds. Weighing each item on a bathroom scale (which we also brought along), we had gone through the agony of many individual decisions to weed the 800 pounds down to 600.

It was with great trepidation that I visited the customs office that February day to claim and declare our personal belongings. Having no idea what the Chinese would allow into the country, I found that my imagination had run to all sorts of extremes—perhaps our books would be confiscated, or partially completed manuscripts that we were both working on tossed out. Anticipating a grueling session, I had written down each item, including the weight and estimated value. The customs agents, six in all, constantly comparing notes and conversing in Chinese, while glancing at me and the list, finally began to interrogate. I expected the worst.

"Are all of these items your own personal belongings?" they inquired.

"Yes, of course," I replied.

"Will you be taking everything back to the United States when you depart from China?"

"Certainly."

"Thank you very much." The lead customs agent handed me the list with a smile. In fact, everyone smiled. There were no more questions. I was speechless.

Nevertheless, we had three more stops, where other officials asked questions and added their stamps to the shipping document. Finally, we went to the cargo holding area, located the box, and brought it to the door outside the Boeing office. We opened it with Chinese tools. The head of the crude hammer kept falling off! The goods inside the box were intact. Items with "up" arrows were upright. This was not usually the case when packing and handling goods in China. Cargo handlers ignored "up" arrows, "fragile" stickers, and all such precautionary signs that might inhibit their manhandling of baggage and cargo.

I removed our two bicycles, which I had dismantled in New York, re-installing the rear-view mirrors and bulb horns. When I blew the horn, my interpreter laughed, saying, "Horns are illegal."

"How do you explain all the honking by the cars and buses?"—worse by far than even in Manhattan on a Saturday afternoon.

"Oh, the officials are doing something about that too," he replied.

Indeed, about a year later, a directive was issued making certain kinds and intensities of horn blowing illegal and punishable by fines. The usual continuous blast of two to five minutes was out—forbidden—replaced by the "two-second sequence, consisting of several small toots." There was an immediate reaction. The decibel level dropped dramatically for the next several weeks, then gradually built up again, but not to the old levels. In the interim, some of the drivers had been converted to saner behavior. Chronic offenders lost their driver's license.

In Beijing, where the right of way was yielded to the driver with the loudest horn and the guts to believe in it, pedestrians did not have a chance. Neither did they seem to care, daring the automobiles to run them down.

As to our bicycle horns, they were quickly stolen, even though we paid to park the bicycles in a special shed at the Beijing Hotel. Our rigid faith in the absolute honesty of the Chinese was seriously jolted. My interpreter was quick to admit that there might be an occasional "bad boy" who would take such items. We noticed that the Chinese were always vigilant in locking their cars, bicycles, and desks. In fact, padlocks in China probably exceeded thermos bottles in total numbers, and were utilized in the most unlikely places. In-plant mail was distributed to individually padlocked, slotted boxes.

Bringing 600 pounds of household items to our single room on the third floor of the Beijing Hotel promised to be a challenge. The Chinese frowned on the practice of adding anything resembling furnishings to the rooms. We solved the problem by taking in one item at a time during daily commuting from the office.

An even greater challenge was finding space in the room. First, the card table. It gave us a place for the second typewriter. Then the three foam cushions, which Beth used on top of the box springs, making it possible for her to sleep. From then on, she slept on a 26-inch wide bed! We reorganized the room in preparation for a long, crowded stay. The CAAC told us that a suite was possible—but to be very patient.

At our three-week anniversary, I was continuing to battle for the suite—and losing. The Chinese were adamant in their goal of moving many of the foreign businessmen out of the Beijing Hotel. During the first blush of normalization, scores of Japanese, American, and European trading companies had moved in, leasing blocks of rooms and in fact taking up all the conference rooms and converting them into office complexes.

Banks, travel agents, steel and oil companies, Hong Kong traders, and a host of miscellaneous businesses zeroed in on China, concentrating in Beijing. The Chinese, recognizing the serious shortage of hotel rooms, and desirous of promoting the tourist trade to gain hard currency quickly, were aghast at the turn of events. I patiently continued to write letters to the manager, but to no avail. I had reached a Chinese stone wall.

At the office, I was becoming established. John Hertel, a Pratt and Whitney engine representative, arrived the last week in February and opened an office in the same building. We began having lunch at the new airport hotel, a bare, austere structure completed at the same time as the new terminal and owned and operated by the CAAC.

One day, as I sat in the restaurant of the new airport hotel, I relaxed for a few moments to recap events. As I sat at a corner table in a sea of round, white-clothed tables with wooden chairs, each covered with a blue slip, the panoply of sameness that pervaded the country drew my attention. Outside, the brilliant sun labored to cut the icy wind. The double-paneled window installations, each equipped with separate hinged panes, provided the necessary protection against the cold. The most striking sound was the lack of sound. At that time there were only eight to ten flights a day from the Capital Airport.

I studied the Chinese eating at a nearby table. Dining is an occasion in China and the larger the group, the better. Rarely, if ever, do you see a Chinese eating alone. The tables are usually round, and the food is brought in large bowls and platters, family style—served by the host or ranking person. I watched their expressions and marveled at the torrent of conversation. The Chinese smiled a lot, if not constantly. The more I observed that feature of the Chinese character, the more it seemed out of place in the austere environment. I concluded that the explanation relates to the tonal language. With many sounds beginning deep in the throat, words are enunciated with the teeth essentially closed. When producing sound, the lips are forced open, and the cheeks assume a natural smile. Thus, as Chinese age, the smile-wrinkles become a permanent feature of their faces.

On my daily trips to the office, I observed the peasants working the land. Agriculture throughout the country has been more finely tuned than anywhere in the world, with the possible exception of Japan. Every square meter is cultivated. Every dry twig, branch, and blade of grass is figuratively counted. In September, the fields around Beijing are planted with winter wheat, which is harvested in late May or early June. Then the ground is quickly prepared for a crop of field corn, an unusual land yield at 40 degrees north latitude. Animal manure and night soil, the human waste carried to the fields in endless caravans of steel drums and tanks, assures the crop yield. In the subtropical region of Chengdu in Sichuan Province, three rice crops are harvested annually.

The year 1979 was the first year of a recent major drought cycle throughout north China, and the reservoirs near Beijing began drying up. Deep wells, drilled extensively in the countryside, were the sole source of water for agriculture. The drought, rated as the worst in one-hundred years, did not break until the summer of 1982. However, some geologists have predicted that a new cycle will begin soon, postulating that the entire north China plain is slowly reverting to desert.

To forestall that possibility, the Chinese have initiated an ambitious plan to irrigate large portions of that parched land with water diverted from the Yangtze River. The Yangtze, its tributaries, and the rivers south of it carry 82 percent of the country's annual runoff, although their drainage area covers only 38 percent of the cultivated land. Reported to have been first proposed as a feasible undertaking by Chairman Mao as early as 1952, the project visualized channeling the water northward for a distance of 1,150 kilometers while raising the level over 40 meters by a series of massive pumping stations.

The "technology curtain" was parting only reluctantly in China. A late 1979 tour of Chinese space technology programs by an AIAA team found extensive and "surprising" high technology progress. Calling it the Sunnyvale, California, counterpart of the United States space technology effort, one member of the team was inspired to comment: "You come away from a fairly modern facility, with good-looking computers, then run into water buffalo dragging a wooden plow." Although tractors were being introduced in larger numbers, the only concession to modern technology by many of the peasants was the rubber tires on the old wooden oxcarts. Bailing wire and rope were their constant companions.

China's greatest pride over the centuries has been its agriculture, the painstaking tilling of the fields and hillsides. Thus, agriculture was given priority as the first of the four modernizations of the New China. Whatever agriculture's announced goals, the peasant's labors are basic to the fabric of society. The determined, happy-faced girl riding the tractor-plow smiles from the one-yuan note of the national currency, in tribute to the marriage of technology with peasant labor.

On the 18th of February, the first snowfall of the season came to Beijing. It was a time for rejoicing. Snow in Beijing in February signifies that spring is near. With a cold north wind prevailing from late October, and a relative humidity of 15 percent, the air is devoid of moisture. When the wind begins its annual shift, an occasional warm front moves in from the south, colliding with the Arctic air to bring a late winter snowstorm.

Although the snowfall was light—one to two inches—it was a godsend. The flakes effectively purged the coal dust from the black cloud that suffocated the city, and for a brief period we enjoyed clean air. Beth had begun to succumb to the dust and was sporting a combination allergic reaction and head cold. In a few days she had developed a hacking cough, and I came down with a fever. As the days passed, the fever refused to leave, and my head and throat were badly congested. I named the malady "Beijing Lung." The term stuck, and I began to hear it often in the ensuing days. Hardly anyone coming to Beijing in winter escaped Beijing Lung.

My body temperature climbed to 102 and hung on. Cold pills and vitamins were of no help. My Chinese hosts became concerned and insisted that I see a doctor. I declined, fearing the medicine and local doctors in equal measure. I decided to grit my teeth and wait until the airplane arrived. Someone would be carrying antibiotics.

CHAPTER 4

ACCORDING TO MY TIME WHEEL, the 747 would be leaving the runway at Everett, Washington, at 8:00 a.m. on February 26, to meet its scheduled rendezvous in Beijing at 2:00 p.m. on the 27th. Crossing the dateline, the travelers on that flight would be losing a day, putting it in the bank until they returned on the eastbound flight. The fourteen hours in the air were just right for the 747, a continent-shrinking airplane that defied the massive span of the Pacific Ocean. The delivery would mark a giant milestone in the Chinese plan to join the technological and commercial airline world.

We had welcomed three snows in Beijing, the third by far the most lasting and beautiful. I was still suffering from Beijing Lung, and Beth was sniffling and wheezing. But spring had inched closer, and some of the bite had gone from the unwelcome north winds.

My urging for a pass to the ramp and loading areas of the airport had continued to fall on deaf ears. The Chinese were still preoccupied with security and secrecy. Foreigners were not to be trusted and were to be constantly kept under disguised surveillance. We were limited to unescorted travel only 50 kilometers from the center of the city. Exceptions were the main tourist attractions near Beijing: the Great Wall, the Ming Tombs, and the site of Peking Man. Everywhere else required a travel pass, each case handled separately and under the jurisdiction of a sponsor—in our case, the CAAC—to make application and generally to accompany the traveler. At a minimum, someone was designated to make contact at the destination.

Everywhere there were armed soldiers—at the entrance to government buildings, at the airport and railroad stations, the canals and bridges, the reservoirs and power stations, even in front of the Beijing Hotel. It was only after 1981 that the soldiers were removed from the hotel environs and replaced by civilians.

Moreover, the Chinese went to great lengths to exclude foreigners from sensitive areas, some of which choices seemed ludicrous. For example, when our driver would stop for gas on the way to work, I would be requested to get out of the car a few blocks from the gas station and wait, while he went on to get the gas.

This separation and exclusion became an accepted way of life. Eventually, we came to anticipate it. Thus, I understood the situation about the airport pass.

"You will not need a pass, because you will always be with us," Mr. Jiang explained one day.

A short time later, with Mr. Jiang, his deputy, Mr. Yu, and me in the car, we approached the gate. First, the driver explained our purpose. The guard stood rigid, expressionless, and determined. He barred our path. Next, Mr. Yu explained. No change. Then the deputy decided that a little authority would be needed, and he joined in the discussion. No avail. Finally, Mr. Jiang, one of the highest CAAC officials at the airport, breathing fire, got out of the car and engaged the guard in a long, arm-waving conversation, apparently convincing him to step aside. I glanced out the rear window when we passed. The guard had a strange expression on his face as he watched us go by. He was afraid that he done the wrong thing—anticipating whatever disciplinary action might be meted out. His orders undoubtedly were simple and direct: no foreigners without

45

passes were allowed to enter the airport ramp or loading areas. He was not permitted to make exceptions.

The next day, Mr. Yu requested that I furnish him with my photograph.

"Why do you need a photograph?" I asked.

"We are going to issue you a pass."

Using my Polaroid camera, I instructed him in taking an instant picture. The next day I was issued the pass. I decided to act quickly, requesting passes for my three compatriots who would be arriving on the airplane. *A few more bricks had been removed from the Chinese wall of secrecy.*

Wednesday, February 27, was a day to remember. On Monday a fresh snowfall, the fourth for the winter, had closed the airport and was followed by a foggy Tuesday, which again closed the single runway for landings. Everything changed on Wednesday. The snow had melted, and the day dawned clear and cold.

I took three cameras to the tarmac: first, my super-8 movie camera to film the approach and landing, then my 35 mm camera to record the taxiing and parking, and, finally, the Polaroid X-70 for personal pictures of the people coming off the plane.

There were disappointments. The U.S. Embassy could not find one of their requested commissary containers that Boeing had carried at no charge. They would miss the Texas grapefruit, California lettuce, Tillamook cheese, and Washington apples. That incident emphasized the differences between the living amenities of the government enclaves and the representatives of foreign industrial concerns in China.

I fared even worse. The plane was overweight at takeoff, resulting in scratching one Embassy container. However, my office supplies and equipment had also been bumped in favor of the other two Embassy containers. My supplies were therefore downgraded to commercial air delivery, and did not arrive until the 15th of March.

The official delivery was made in Beijing, an unusual procedure. If delivered in Seattle, the usual custom, the plane, as Chinese property, would have been vulnerable to court confiscation attempts, in payment of old claims by American creditors.

After having taken simulator training at the Boeing plant in Seattle, the Chinese flight crews came home on the airplane. Three Boeing maintenance technicians were also on board, completing my support contingent. But the most welcome sight was the Boeing sales director, Jim Chorlton, who had been to China many times and discovered the cure for Beijing Lung —tetracycline. After taking the treatment, I returned to the living.

Everyone coming to Beijing had an intense desire to be located at the Beijing Hotel. The Boeing technicians had been counting on it and were dismayed to learn that they would actually be sent to the Friendship Hotel, a sprawling complex of buildings in the northwest section of the city, with no air-conditioning, poor heating, and few private telephones. Because of that bad news, I gave the technicians the next day off. On Friday we put the pieces back together. Then the Chinese insisted that we take a short rest for the weekend.

"One more day to relax until all hell breaks loose," were my thoughts on Sunday morning, reflecting on the pent-up feelings of my colleagues at the Friendship Hotel, coupled with the cold, the wind, and the paucity of spare parts and handling equipment. Seldom had Boeing employees been exposed to a place as rigorous as China.

On Monday the Chinese signed the papers and officially took ownership of the airplane. There were a few minor flight pickups from the delivery flight, which were quickly handled. Replacement parts were ordered from the home plant on a critical priority.

I immediately received a barrage of complaints about the

Friendship Hotel. My only solution was to transfer the team to the CAAC Hotel at the airport. There were only five two-room suites in the entire complex, and we contracted for three of those for the duration. The cost doubled, but we needed satisfied people.

The Boeing maintenance technicians were on six-month temporary assignments, on single status, but allowed to return to the U.S. at the end of three months to visit their families. My own status was a permanent assignment, a minimum of two years' duration with a home leave at the end of eighteen months.

The suites were nicely arranged, boasting refrigerators and television sets. The *wentis* were lack of produce to put in the refrigerators, and the single TV program was in Chinese. Isolation, the principal drawback, was essentially complete, with downtown 30 kilometers away. Moreover, downtown offered little of the amenities to which Americans were accustomed. Other than the Friendship Store for limited shopping, and the department store on Wangfujing street, where local Chinese were jammed curb to curb seven days a week, there was nothing. There were no night clubs, no discos, in fact no dancing of any kind. Above all, a perceived disaster by single men, there were no available women. The Chinese girls were strictly off limits. Sightseeing trips to the Forbidden City, Temple of Heaven, Beihai Park, the Summer Palace, and a few other points of interest would be exhausted in a matter of weeks. A grim outlook!

Training of the flight crews began the following week. The Boeing instructors stayed for two weeks and trained twelve 747 crews. Everything went as smooth as silk—except for the tires. The runway had half-inch-deep lateral grooves to minimize the effects of icing in the winter. The multiple touch-and-go landings required for training chewed giant chunks out of the tires, and suddenly there was a shortage.

Anticipating the need for additional tires, I inquired as to the whereabouts of the spares. Mr. Zhang Guangrong, Chief Provisioning Engineer, with an encyclopedic mind, came to the office to discuss the situation. "Mr. Zhang," I advised, "we will need quite a large number of spare tires because of the rough runway."

"I can order them from Hong Kong on a rush basis."

"Are you saying that the CAAC did not order any spare tires?"

"Oh, yes, we ordered several sets, but they are with the main group of spare parts."

"You mean on the ship?"

"Yes, most of the spare parts are on the ship."

It was difficult—inconceivable, in fact—for me to imagine that no spare parts had been flown in previous to, or simultaneously with, the delivery flight. But as I came to know the Chinese better, and understood their rigid petty-cash attitude, it was no longer surprising.

In order to minimize tire attrition, the touch-and-go landings were to be conducted at Tianjin (Tientsin), scarcely 200 kilometers away, thus reducing the Beijing landings to one a day. The strategy worked. Nevertheless, before that idea was implemented, all 16 main wheel tires required replacement. The extra spares did not arrive from Hong Kong until the following afternoon, causing a full day's delay in the training schedule. Where most airlines would have fretted and fumed over the time loss, the Chinese hardly noticed.

Next, it was discovered that there was no wrench for removing the wheel nut. A quick check of the records revealed that the Chinese had opted to make the wrench locally, but had not yet directed anyone to do it. We sketched up a rough drawing, and the machine shop welded a wrench from steel plate. Another day and a half were lost from the training schedule.

On Saturday, Boeing Chairman Mr. "T" Wilson arrived to

meet with Chinese officials and participate in a symbolic key-transfer ceremony. A highlight on Sunday evening was a huge banquet in the Great Hall of the People in Tiananmen Square. Tiananmen Square cornerstones the history of the Chinese Revolution and the new Communistic nation. It was there that the late Chairman Mao proclaimed the founding of the People's Republic on October 1, 1949. Daily, from morning to night, the Square teems with people. Located in the center of Beijing, directly in front of the Forbidden City, the Square is the largest in the world, covering 40 hectares (99 acres). A half million people can fit into its boundaries. On the west, it is flanked by the colossus of marble and stone, the Great Hall of the People. On the south stands Mao's Tomb, and on the east a museum. Immediately to the south of the Tomb is Qianmen Gate, one of the few remaining vestiges of the wall that has surrounded the city of Beijing since its earliest beginnings.

In the early days of the People's Republic, a central goal was to do away with all things old. The "Four Olds" were old things, old ideas, old customs, and old habits. In 1959, the wall was dismantled, and a row of apartment houses began to rise in its place.

Ever mindful of our personal needs, and recognizing the paucity of recreation in Beijing, our Chinese hosts continued to offer a trip to the Great Wall and the Ming Tombs, relatively close to each other and both within 80 kilometers of the city. However, having heard of the fierce winds at the Wall, we declined to go until the weather improved. Instead, we accepted the opportunity to tour the Forbidden City.

A succession of 24 emperors resided in the Imperial Palace of the Forbidden City from the mid-14th to the early 20th century. The Palace is now open as the Palace Museum, attracting thousands of visitors each day with its magnificent architecture and collections of art objects.

The buildings of the Forbidden City, housing 9,000 rooms, constitute the most complete assemblage of traditional Chinese architecture still in existence. The Palace area, rectangular in shape and 720,000 square meters (178 acres) in size, is surrounded by walls 10 meters high and a moat 52 meters wide. Each of the four corners of the walls has a tower with a ridged roof covered with glazed tiles.

The Palace construction was undertaken in 1406 by the third emperor of the Ming Dynasty, Cheng Zu. It is believed that 100,000 artisans and 1 million workmen toiled on the project for fourteen years. The complex consists of many separate buildings, all imposing structures in their own right and connected by stone walkways, adorned on either hand with statues and fountains.

After entering Meridian Gate on the Square at the south entrance, one passes through the Gate of Supreme Harmony, the Hall of Supreme Harmony, the Hall of Central Harmony, and the Hall of Preserving Harmony.

Behind the Hall of Central Harmony is a huge stone slab 16.57 meters long, 3.07 meters wide, and 1.7 meters thick, and weighing over 200 tons. This stone slab is representative of those quarried in the mountains southwest of Beijing and brought to the place of construction during the winter. Wells were dug at half-kilometer intervals along the way, and water drawn from them was poured over the roads to freeze. The slabs were transported on flat-bottomed boats over the ice.

After one passes the Hall of Preserving Harmony, the Gate of Heavenly Purity is reached, beyond which is the Palace proper, where the Ming and Qing emperors lived and conducted their daily governmental duties. The empresses' bedchambers are also located there. Beyond the Gate stands the Hall of Heavenly Purity, the Hall of Union, and the Hall of Earthly Tranquility. While Purity and Tranquility served as the emperors' quarters, Union was the depository for the 25 jade seals of government. Amid all the imposing stone and finery lived hundreds of imperial concubines and thousands of attendants.

Life within the Imperial Palace, resplendent in its excesses of gold, silver, and jade, was marked by idleness, extravagance, and intrigue. The cost of a single meal served to the Empress was estimated as sufficient to feed 5,000 peasants. Therein grew the seeds of revolution that eventually led to the Communistic takeover and the new China.

During the emperor's reign, ordinary citizens were ordered to keep their distance from the Palace, hence the name "Forbidden City." At night no male person other than the emperor was allowed inside the walls, only the eunuchs.

In a nation where allegiance to an unseen ruler was complete, an imposter need only to manage to kill him and capture the Imperial Seal to achieve absolute control. This centuries-old trait of the Chinese people later made it easy for Chairman Mao quickly to establish a God-like image and become "leader for 10,000 years."

Every day I witnessed the stultifying legacy of millennia of blind attention to directives and edicts.

CHAPTER 5

Spring simply refused to make its appearance that winter of 1980, with still another three inches of wet snow falling in March. On the flight line, we had again exhausted our supply of tires. Training flights ceased for two more days. Although the officials expressed concern, the Chinese mechanics were unperturbed. It gave them an opportunity for longer *xuixis* and more time to play their favorite card game, *si shi fen* (forty points).

With April standing in the wings, and the inauguration of regular commercial 747 service scheduled for April 1, time was growing short. Abruptly the Chinese announced a route-proving flight from Beijing to Shanghai on the 24th of March. We were all invited to go along—first class.

Flight CA 151, replacing the regular 707 flight that day, actually took paying passengers. They merely switched planes on the regularly scheduled flight. It was smooth and uneventful. We flew over the 2,903-mile-long Huanghe (Yellow River), historically known as "China's Sorrow" because of the crushing floods over the centuries. Flowing through nine provinces and autonomous regions, it is second in length only to the Changjiang (Yangtze) River, draining an area the size of Texas, inhabited by 100 million people.

Shanghai turned out a hero's welcome on a pleasant spring day, the greening of the countryside a startling contrast to cold, lifeless Beijing. The Chinese, always gracious hosts, served a sumptuous lunch at the Shanghai airport. For the return trip, with all the first-class seats occupied by paying passengers, we retreated to our usual habitat in the economy section. Since everything in China is done by numbers, levels, stages, and degrees, the seats were sold by row from front to aft, with no attention made to aisle or window, smoking or non-smoking. At least this procedure made counting the passengers easy—all the empties were in neat rows in the back. In time, the airline introduced seating niceties similar to their competitors in the West.

Television cameras were everywhere, and I found myself staring into blinding lights at every turn, prodded with questions by Chinese journalists. Most of the questions had easy answers. "How many passengers does the airplane carry? How high will it fly? Can it fly halfway around the world?" But I avoided answering a few, for example, "How much does the airplane cost?"

The airline officials were so pleased by the performance of the airplane that they substituted the 747 for the regular 707 flight to Guangzhou (Canton) that same evening. Flushed with success, they were treating it as a new toy, and, according to their philosophy, nothing could go wrong—simply because it was new. Easy!

On the following Wednesday, they decided to repeat the Monday operation. But alas, a fuel leak developed. A minor leak, but difficult of access, and all fuel leaks must always be repaired prior to further flights.

The problem proved to be that of a faulty O-ring, but the Chinese had no spares. They tried an O-ring from a Trident airplane. It looked the same. The leak worsened. The Trident O-ring was slightly different in size. An emergency order was telexed to Japan Airlines in Tokyo. In the meantime, it was discovered that the 707 had an O-ring that was the correct size—a Boeing standard.

The episode was damaging to Chinese credibility, and a first step in losing passenger confidence. The Wednesday flight had been announced with fanfare, all passengers having been informed that the 3:30 fight to Guangzhou would be with the sparkling new 747. When passengers arrived at the gate, they discovered the same old 707 airplane.

Training flights continued. On Friday a shaft sheared on one of the hydraulic pumps. The pump was replaced with a new unit, fortunately one of the critical spares that was included in the air shipment.

By coincidence, I had made a last-minute decision to go to the office the following morning—Saturday—normally a day off. A leak had suddenly developed in the hydraulic pressure line leading from the newly installed pump. I suspected that it had been damged by the use of improper tools on the previous installation, but could not prove it. We were able to cannibalize an identical hose assembly from the quick engine change (QEC) kit, thus solving the problem.

That episode cooled the Chinese' enthusiasm still further. They were discovering some hard facts. Modern airplanes were exceedingly complex, and in spite of having new machines with greater built-in reliability, spare parts and the tools to install them were essential. Deciding to play it safe, they parked the airplane for two days in preparation for the inaugural flight to Paris on the following Tuesday, April 1, 1980.

After the Paris flight, I was reminded of the old medical joke, "The operation was a success, but the patient died." The flight was outstanding—only minor technical problems. However, where it counted most, in paying passengers, it was a dismal failure, having a total of 125 outbound and only 36 on the return. With break-even at about 135 in the 291-passenger airplane, the CAAC had a lot of image-building to do.

The Thursday flight to Tokyo was better, nearly break-even. Friday was maintenance day—no flights—and the first time everyone was required to work as a team under operating conditions. They did a creditable job.

The Chinese invited us to an acrobatic show on Friday night. It was a smash hit. For two solid hours the Beijing troupe, who had performed throughout the world, astounded the predominantly foreign audience. There were jugglers, magicians, and clowns, but it was the amazingly nimble acrobatic girls, with their feather touch and incredible balance, who stole the show. The cost was 60 *fen* per ticket, equivalent to 38 cents in United States money. Shows in China had to be low-priced in order for the local people to afford them. With urban workers earning an average salary of 40 yuan ($25 U.S.) per month, there was little for entertainment. The Chinese, ringing the balcony, seemed more interested in watching the unfamiliar foreigners on the main floor below than the activities on the stage.

Celebrating sixty days in the inscrutable Chinese People's Republic, I felt I was beginning to understand something of the environment. Of course, five years later, I was much better informed, and still learning. The country is so large and its history so intimidating that understanding builds slowly. I could identify only small islands of technical literacy, with those unconnected havens of technological endeavor struggling to break the barriers that separated them.

The first impediment to progress is a language that suffers from its most notable attributes: both artistry and primitiveness. The second is the decision-making process, where the most minor item passes in a linear mode to the top of the organization. Factories may stand side by side, engaged in making different parts for the same machine, and yet operate in total ignorance of each other's activities. Everything goes up, across the top, and back down the other side. For the airline, a business entity that by nature should be capable of rapidly responding to a volatile environment, the linear decision process was a serious handicap.

On April 6 Easter came without notice. There were no tears of joy in the eyes of the Chinese, no glad tidings on their lips. The pitifully small foreign community observed the day with their own inner thoughts and prayers. In a country where work is a religion in itself, and a six-day week the norm, stores and shops are open the year around, with the exception of the three major holidays: Spring Festival, Labor Day, and National Day.

Nevertheless, as a result of the revisions to the constitution in 1978 and 1982, more Chinese were venturing back to the churches. In Beijing the handful of converts was steadily growing. Hardly noticed by the teeming crowds of pedestrians and cyclists on Dongdanjie, where the main Protestant congregation met, the faithful few turned in to the church. From a scant 100 in early February 1980, the crowds of Easter Sunday bulged to over 300. Two services were necessary for the first time in recent memory.

Even though the revival of the Beijing Christian Church represented only a tiny island among the 9 million inhabitants, we noticed a change on that first Easter. A few young people were present, sprinkled among the old, an omen of the passing of the faith to a new generation. By mid-1984 it was reported that there were 3 million Protestants in China.[1]

Beth and I sat in wooden chairs, in the unheated building, somewhere between 45 degrees F. and freezing. The congregation, in heavy coats, scarves, and multiple sweaters, responded lustily to the call of the pump organ, seeming to feel the need for warming their voices in the chill of the morning.

The scripture was from Ezekiel, the Gospel of John, and Romans, and the hymns "Christ the Lord is Risen Today"

---

[1] *China Daily,* August 7, 1984.

and "The Strife is Over" shook the ancient walls as the Chinese and foreign voices joined in a common tune. In the street below, the urgent, impatient automobiles honked their way through the swarms of bicycles, and an occasional motorcycle buzzed above the din.

During communion, quiet meditation was debauched by the rude whir of movie cameras in the hands of curious foreigners, and a flash of bulbs reflected from the minister's face as he intoned the prayer.

I marveled at the number of lame, blind, and infirm. An aged woman, the skin of her face creased by the winds of eighty winters, held a four-inch-diameter magnifying glass in one hand as she read her worn Bible.

The altar was adorned with flowers and plants from nearby greenhouses: a calla lily, a white geranium, and a green bamboo shoot—small but significant tokens of the tribute to the risen Lord. So there, as everywhere, Christ lives, and Easter reminds all those in whom may yet be found a scrap of response, that creation is constant and deathless.

Thus, in the space of a single week, we witnessed two quite disparate milestones—the successful inauguration flights to Paris and Tokyo with the new 747 jumbo airplane, and the first Christian Easter service in Beijing since the Cultural Revolution—both boding well for progress in China.

CHAPTER 6

BY THE THIRD WEEK of April the 747 was beginning to attract larger passenger loads. The weekly flight from Beijing to Guangzhou was full—291 passengers—including some foreigners. Tourist influx began a noticeable acceleration in April, a welcome sight to the airline officials because full loads of local people would not produce break-even revenue on domestic flights.

As with everything in China, foreigners were charged substantially more. Except on international flights, the Chinese traveled at 40 percent of full fare. When I discussed this disparity with my Chinese friends, they laughed, shrugged, and said, "But Americans make more, and should therefore pay more." Thus, a one-way ticket from Beijing to Shanghai aboard CAAC airplanes cost $32 U.S. for Chinese citizens and over $80 for foreigners.

Pricing differences were not limited to the airline. Throughout China, vast differences existed in the prices of goods and services, depending upon who was doing the buying. At the time, Scott Seligman, Beijing Representative of the National Council on United States–China Trade, took the Chinese to task concerning their pricing practices.[1] "In a nation where friendship stores are set up to cater exclusively to foreign guests,

---

[1] "China's High 'Friendship' Prices for Foreigners," Scott D. Seligman, *Asian Wall Street Journal,* June 23, 1982.

and friendship is toasted at nearly every banquet, Westerners have begun to refer derisively to friendship prices."

Following Seligman's admonition, a top tourism official in China defended the policies of charging foreigners double or triple the prices charged to Chinese nationals. Mr. Wang Yueyi, Deputy Director of Tourism and Travel, stated: "The price and salary policy of China is very different from Western nations. In the West there are high prices and high salaries, and in China there are low prices and low salaries because of Chinese government subsidies."[2]

Since winter had been reluctant to leave, we were amazed at how abruptly summer came. Spring in Beijing consists of three weeks in April. The Chinese handle the season change in their patented bureaucratic fashion, deciding that winter begins on November 15 and ends on March 15, coincident with the dates for turning the coal stoves on and off. Shortly after winter ended, the air began to clear, and Beth and I returned to full health.

The bare, lifeless terrain on the road to the airport suddenly sprang into life, with tender new leaves magically appearing everywhere and the forsythia bursting forth into gorgeous yellow cascades.

Spring brought still another major event in the practiced cadence of the Chinese year: tree planting. Throughout China, millions of trees were being planted each spring in a drive for reforestation. For thousands of years, timber supplies had yielded to the voracious appetites of wood-burning stoves. Then, during the early years of the People's Republic, the State encouraged people to cut down the remaining forests to plant more grain. Droughts and dust storms followed, reservoirs dried up, and the water table in the deep wells began a rapid fall.

[2] "Why Tourists Pay More," *South China Morning Post,* August 4, 1982.

Tree planting campaigns started in the 1950s, and China's new forestry law, implemented in 1979, revived this effort. In the Beijing area alone, 6,500 trees and shrubs were planted during the first two weeks of April 1980. In 1981 and 1982, plantings increased. By that time entire mountainsides had been reforested. Special police stations were set up to arrest people damaging or destroying forests. In Fujian Province, it has been reported that local people's courts punished 545 offenders over a period of two years, of whom two were sentenced to death.[3]

However, as in many other situations, the Chinese were ambivalent in handling trees. In spite of the national drive to reforest, certain trees were offered special treatment at the expense of others. To protect a particular variety at the airport, for instance, wind barriers were constructed around each individual tree every autumn and removed the following spring. Each of these constructions consumed seven to ten other trees, sacrificed as poles to build the braces for protection from the 60-knot winter winds.

During the short "three-week" spring, the weather was very unsettled, and a sudden cold snap in mid-April proved the Chinese adage that Mr. Yu had reminded me of so many times—take off clothing slowly in the spring and add it slowly in the fall, one layer at a time. I had already changed to summer suits, and was nearly freezing in the bitter north wind as I cycled to the bank.

The cold, wind, and dust combined to make maintenance of the airplanes nearly impossible on the unprotected ramp. A hangar, designed to house one 747, delayed by cost considerations and a torturous approval process, had not yet been committed to construction. A temporary building measuring ten feet by eighteen feet was the sole repository for the tools, service items, and maintenance manuals. The building rapidly

---

[3] *China Daily,* August 24, 1984.

acquired the name "maintenance shack," a term the Chinese began to repeat. It was simply the best they had at the time. With a sudden burst of activity, the Chinese started construction of the hangar in May, announcing that it would be ready for occupancy by winter.

A few weeks earlier, Beth and I had made another stab at getting a suite. I decided to take the direct approach, and so made an official appointment with the manager. He was cordial but unyielding. When he recognized my persistence, he fell back to the old Chinese trick of disclaiming responsibility. The allocations were made by the First Service Bureau, he announced. They controlled every hotel room in the entire city of Beijing. One giant Ouji board! That began to explain why the CAAC, our sponsor, was faring so badly and could not even make reservations at the hotels. In fact they never knew which hotel a guest would be assigned until the day of arrival. The allocation of rooms was tied directly to the issuance of visas. If no rooms were available, no visas were approved—a mechanism to manage the inflow of foreign visitors. In those days, the Chinese were taking unfair blame for being recalcitrant and even unfriendly, when the problem was actually the shortage of accommodations. In 1983, the hotel availability bottleneck began to ease, and 9,580 rooms were promised for Beijing alone by 1985, up from less than 3,000 in 1980.

After buckets of tea and profuse cordialities, we left the manager's office with the impression that the only conduit was via our sponsor, and that option looked pretty dismal. We resigned ourselves to a long wait.

During that week, our falling spirits were lightened by four packages of mail from the U.S. Nothing had arrived for the previous ten days. But we were occasionally garnering a newspaper from an airplane after its arrival from Tokyo or

Paris—sometimes real honest-to-God American newspapers. Even the classified ads looked good!

One day, some stray strawberries were left in the galley on the plane. Fresh strawberries! I ate a nice, juicy, red berry and set one aside on my desk in the office for Beth, but, alas, by the end of the day it had disappeared.

On Sunday we visited the Xin Xiao Hotel for the "best Western food in Beijing." We had something called "frillet mignon." This was neither a misspelling nor a filet mignon; rather, it was the usual tough local meat served elsewhere in Beijing, only with different trimmings. At least we were able to get our first order of mashed potatoes.

The following week I received several inquiries concerning the "movie problem" on the CAAC 747 airplane. The Chinese had been operating the 747 for several weeks and still there were no on-board movies. For the long flights to Paris, about thirteen hours, foreigners considered movies a must—all other international airlines offered them. In an earlier decision, the CAAC had opted to have the earphones locally manufactured, assigning the task to a Shanghai factory. As usual, delivery was far behind schedule. For China, delay and missed schedules were standard—in fact, accepted as a necessary part of doing business. If there was a choice between acceleration by working overtime or postponement, the Chinese would always choose postponement.

We also continued to be plagued by a shortage of spare parts. In those first few months the CAAC operated without a spare engine, an unheard-of practice for most airlines. The four spare engines that had been ordered from Pratt/Whitney had been consigned to shipment by sea. The first engine was not due to arrive until the end of May, on the proverbial slow boat to China, via the Panama Canal. The Chinese seemed unworried, taking the position that "the airplane was new," and thus nothing should go wrong. There was the tacit assumption that Boeing should do the worrying.

During April we gained an additional interpreter to support Mr. Yu. Mr. Ming, the new man, was a hair-trigger type, hopping around like a cricket and fretting over every detail. On the 18th of April, upon my arrival at the office, I found him in a very nervous state.

"Mr. Bauer," he excitedly announced, "something has collided with the airplane!"

With a quickening pulse, I noticed the concern and fear on Mr. Ming's face and asked, "What sort of collision?"

"I think the cargo loader hit the airplane."

"And what damage was done?"

"I don't know," he said, pacing nervously around the office. "I believe there is a hole in the airplane."

Considering our less than perfect communication, I had visions of major structural damage. Finally, Mr. Ming became more coherent. "The cargo door was in the open position, and the loader hit it," he explained.

Heading for the ramp, I expected to find a badly crumpled door and an AOG (Airplane On Ground) for several days or weeks.

Upon my arrival at the airplane, I was relieved to find only minor damage. The loader had bent the door-to-body fairing, but had not touched the main structure. It would be an easy fiberglass layup and could be temporarily repaired with "speed tape."

A Chinese maintenance technician had run the loader into the door. When I inquired what happened to him, I was told that he stopped the machine, jumped off, and headed for the Great Wall. The Chinese treated the incident as a joke, in spite of the fact that "accident-prone" people were usually transferred to another job—most probably to the rice fields as common laborers. The term was "re-programming through labor."

Another aspect bothered me even more—the lack of a realization of the value of the equipment that the workers were handling. The idea of working with a $50 million airplane was beyond the scope of their comprehension.

That day was notable for still another reason. The weatherman, no more accurate in China than elsewhere, had predicted a clear, balmy 70 degrees F, but before the day was over we had a howling dust storm. By 2:00 p.m., the sun disappeared and visibility dropped to 400 feet. All flights were canceled. The airport was closed. The dreaded dust-storm season of late April and early May had begun, an annual occurrence because of the shift of the prevailing winds from north to south.

We had visions of the Gobi Desert descending upon us. The air was filled with a suspension of fine dust particles. Layers of dust settled like a coating of new-fallen snow—yellow, gritty dust. As the afternoon wore on, the intensity of the winds increased to force level of 7 or 8 (10 is a hurricane). The Chinese disappeared from the streets—pedestrians, cyclists, and all—fleeing to the comparative safety of their heavy-roofed stone, brick, and mud buildings.

During the dust season, thousands of tons of Gobi Desert sand blew eastward over northern China and was carried upward into the jet stream, where it traveled all the way to Japan and on into the Pacific. It could have been worse. In the spring of 1287, Beijing suffered its worst dust storm in history, when yellow dust fell for seven days and nights, by which time the drifts of powder were more than two meters deep in places. Cattle were buried where they stood.[4]

Assigning force levels to the winds was a reminder of the

---

[4] *Ibid.*, May 5, 1984.

rigorous bureaucratic system that prevailed in China. All walks of life, all people, all activities, were included. The waiters and waitresses in the dining rooms of the hotels had numbers instead of names. The tables were numbered, as well as the courses on the menus. The year was divided according to the lunar calendar into 24 two-week periods. Each period had certain instructions for the farmers concerning planting, pruning, cultivating, fertilizing, and harvesting. Products were numbered. Paper napkins possessed a grade, size, and color, all according to code. In the hotel, it took eight individuals to make up a room. Beginning about 7:30 a.m., they came trooping in by ones and twos: one to clean the bathroom, one to take out the dirty linen, another two to make the beds, still another to bring the fresh thermos bottles of hot and cooled boiled water. Specific individuals emptied the wastebaskets. Vacuuming the carpets was a rare event, but it was usually accomplished by someone specializing in vacuuming. Waxing the hallways was likewise a specialized job.

If a light bulb burned out, an "electrician" was called. If the sink stopped up, a "plumber" was called. Leaky faucets seemed to be in a category that did not require, nor warrant, fixing. In spite of the constant railing in the newspapers and on the radio to conserve water, energy, raw materials—in fact everything—little attention was paid to faulty plumbing.

Salaries were according to classifications; factory workers, office workers, maids, drivers, etc. (Peasants shared in the incomes of the coops of which they were members.) Everyone retired at the same age (in theory); pensions were tied to the wage received while employed. People were told where to live—without a choice. They were assigned to jobs and careers without being consulted. When a new apartment house was built, the State made up a list of the most appropriate tenants, and those people were invited to move in. They never refused. Most probably their block of old homes had been scheduled for destruction. In short, the life of each person was totally regulated from birth until the body was carted away to the state crematorium.

Materials were allocated according to strict formulas. I noted that a regular quota of soap and toilet paper was supplied to the bathroom. If we brought our own soap and toilet paper in from the outside, which we often did because of the poor quality of the local products, the soap piled up in the bathroom and the toilet paper rolls stacked up. When we first arrived, there was no procedure for changing the allocation except via a formal re-allocation process. Before the year was over, however, those minor decisions had been delegated to the "floor boys." The situation changed by 180 degrees. Unaccustomed to making decisions, and with the incentive of the edict removed, the floor boys usually forgot to replenish staple items. Invariably, we had to make a specific request on each occasion, sometimes repeatedly.

For the Chinese, ration cards were required for most purchases. There was an allocation list for bicycles. Cotton materials were limited to a single purchase a year, with eight meters of cloth allowed for each family. Even food was rationed, with long queues waiting. Often food supplies ran out before the queue was satisfied, causing the losers to return again and again. In the autumn, when millions of kilos of cabbage arrived from the fields, each family was allowed to purchase 9.9 kilos of the number-one grade, with no restrictions on the lower grades. Fortunately for foreigners, there were no ration or quota restrictions except for cotton fabric in Chinese shops.

As U.S. wages go, the Chinese were at rock bottom. With peasants earning 15 yuan ($10 U.S.) a month when we arrived in 1980, the scales graded up to professionals. University professors were separated into 12 ranks, with salaries from 65 to 360 yuan per month, perhaps representing the top scale for anyone in the country, with the exception of the very high government officials.

I was amazed to learn that the captain of the 747 airplane was paid 120 yuan a month, roughly $80 U.S., compared to the $80,000 to $100,000 a year paid by many international airlines.

However, with the modernization policies of "free markets" for farm produce and substitution of taxation for government profit-taking, the earnings of peasants and factory workers alike increased substantially during the next four years.[5]

People were organized into units, and everyone had to belong. The units formed into larger groups called brigades. The entire country was organized like a huge army. I particularly noticed the brigades working along the route to the airport. The tree-cutting brigades were hard at work during the winter and early spring. They literally massacred the stately trees growing along the 30-kilometer stretch of road. The weeping willows and cottonwood trees, mostly in the range of a foot in diameter, were being cut back just above the branching point, converted into little more than ugly stumps. The cutters were quite careless, letting bark tear away and not using a tree-healing substance on the huge scars. I referred to them as tree butchers. More amazing, they were still busily cutting in late March and early April, with the leaves already coming out.

No one seemed to care if the trees died. That would make work for the brigades assigned to removing dead trees—and, of course, work for the tree-planting brigades the following year.

Toward the end of April I received a call from the customs officials at the airport. I was informed that the microfilm reader-printer that was part of my office equipment was "fully duti-

[5]*Ibid.*, March 2, 1983.

able'' and that I should make arrangements to pay the duty forthwith. Since it was Saturday, I promised to discuss it with the CAAC and meet with the customs agents on the following Monday.

The machine in question had been shipped from the U.S. with my office supplies, and the Chinese customs officials had been vigilant in recording every item. The reader-printer cost $4,500 U.S., and I was told the duty would be one-half of that sum. Outraged, I decided to test the Chinese system for flexibility and, above all, to establish a precedent. Otherwise, in the future we would be paying duty on everything.

First, I notified the interpreters that I did not plan to pay duty, since the machine was brought in for the sole purpose of supporting the Chinese airline. It was not being used for personal business, would not be resold in China, and would eventually be returned to the United States. The interpreters agreed that my argument was reasonable, but, nevertheless, cautioned that customs agents were very powerful and hard to deal with.

I then requested an audience with the CAAC authorities, and Mr. Tao, the Communist Party Secretary for the CAAC group, listened to my story. "I decline to pay any duty whatsoever," I announced for openers. "I'll send the machine back to the United States. Then I'll ask the CAAC to furnish an equivalent machine to support the airline. After all, it is used exclusively to help me solve problems for the CAAC."

Mr. Tao listened intently. "I'll take it up with the customs officials," he concluded. A few days later, he reported that the customs had certain rules and could not make exceptions. However, in this case they were prepared to deviate a little and would accept a deposit. The deposit would be an insurance that we would actually take the machine out in the future. That way, the law could be followed. Otherwise, they said, I was asking them to break the law.

That experience reinforced my conviction of the hard-and-fast rules in China. No one was allowed to take personal initiative; no judgments could be made; and no individual logic could be applied to specific cases, no matter how absurd the rule.

I inquired as to the amount of the deposit and was informed that 1,000 yuan—a round, arbitrary number—would be satisfactory. The following weekend, against my letter of credit, I withdrew 1,000 yuan from the Bank of China. Taking the bundle of ten yuan bills, the largest denomination issued at the time, to the customs office, I offered to make the deposit.

Mr. Tao had preceded me into the office, a necessary gesture in Chinese transactions, to set the stage and make certain no one would lose face. He quickly returned and announced that everything was in order. Customs would accept the deposit. The agent made out a receipt with four carbons and presented the original to me.

"But you have not listed the exchange rate," I complained, handing it back. Everyone had unbelieving looks on their faces. Such audacity! I explained via my interpreter that the exchange rate should be written on the receipt so that when it was redeemed I would receive the same number of U.S. dollars in equivalent yuan as I had deposited. Obviously, the agent was not schooled in finance. He pointed to the safe and informed me that the bundle of bills would be placed inside, and the exact same bundle returned to me at the time I departed, perhaps years later.

I insisted that he call the bank, inquire for the exchange rate for the day, and write it on the receipt. Confused, the agent went to his superior for support, who in turn called the highest official at the airport. In those days, the highest positions were held by peasants, probably Party members, whose sole qualification was their revolutionary zeal. After a vigorous conference, they decided in my favor, apparently on the premise that it could do no harm to have the exchange rate written on the receipt. They called the bank. After determining the rate, they wrote the number on my original and handed it back to me. Quickly returning it for the second time, I requested they put the carbons back in and complete all the copies.

From their incredulous expressions, I was certain they believed I had lost my mind. Nevertheless, they reluctantly complied. Shaking their heads, they took the stack of bills and deposited it in the safe, meticulously indicating how it would be left there and locked away for the duration.

"I'm surprised that they keep the money in the safe," I confided to Mr. Yu on the way out. "I would have expected it to go to the bank to gain interest."

"Oh, they don't pay any attention to interest, Mr. Bauer. They have over 40,000 yuan in that safe."

CHAPTER 7

THE HEADPHONES ARRIVED from the factory in Shanghai during the first week in May. When I came to the ramp on maintenance day, everything was quiet. No one was visible, and no work was being done. Climbing the stand into the airplane, I found the entire maintenance crew sitting in the passenger seats, headphones in place—watching Superman!

Movies proved to be a difficult problem for the Chinese. They were becoming aware of the importance that modern travelers attached to movies, and the impact they had on airline competition. However, the rules as to what was acceptable were very strict. In the old days, before normalization, it had been sufficient to sing revolutionary songs, inviting the passengers to join in.

After screening a large number of movies, the Chinese authorities selected "Superman," "Buck Rogers," and "The Muppets." The others were "not suitable." For the next several months, passengers on the CAAC flights were given a solid diet of those three movies.

While in Beijing, I was also making my own movies of the Chinese going about their daily activities in the city and the surrounding countryside. Limited to a radius of fifty kilometers from the city's center, I made the best of it. Taking my American-made bicycle and my super-8 movie camera, I was able to capture the sweep of activities of their daily lives.

While I made my own movies, I reflected on the Chinese movie dilemma. The difficulty in coming to grips with the issue was typical of the dichotomies created by the modernization program. The Communist Party was facing a two-headed dragon. On the one hand, it maintained control of people's lives, shaping their thoughts and goals, while, on the other, it tried to provide sufficient freedom to assimilate Western technology.

Deng Xiaoping had already expressed his concern that the Party had too many members, and he was determined to reduce it. Nevertheless, it continued to grow. Xinhua News Agency reported in April 1980 that the Communist Party had approximately 19 million members at the beginning of the Cultural Revolution, and the number doubled during the period to about 38 million. However, on August 19, 1982, *China Daily* reported that more than 4.6 million new members had been admitted in the previous four years.

In 1949, when the People's Republic was proclaimed, the Party had 4.4 million members. Thus, with the overall population of China doubling between 1949 and 1979, the Party increased nine-fold during the same period. *China Daily* stated that "these new members are people with high political consciousness and professional abilities."

Vice Chairman Deng Xiaoping's program for control and motivation of the masses started before a person was born, or even conceived. First and foremost were the strict new regulations for population control—initially disclosed in Guangdong Province—which lay down a whole range of financial, administrative, and social penalties against parents who aggravated China's population crisis by having more than two children, or who reneged on a reward-bearing commitment to have only one. These Draconian measures were seen by Deng and his colleagues as a must, even though grain production in 1981 was rising faster than the population and in 1982 reached an all-time high.

The idea was being advanced, and was becoming a benchmark, to achieve a decrease in the country's population in the 21st century—a feasible goal if most couples would bear only one child. Indeed, the favorable ratio of grain production to increase in population was one of the significant results of the recent reduction in births. In 1985, a ranking UN official in charge of population activities in China said China has carried out "an effective population policy" and has done "an excellent job" in reducing its population growth rate from 2 percent to 1.1 percent in the past 10 years.[1] Thus, the goal of holding the total population to 1.2 billion by the year 2000 seems possible.

Another serious impediment to meeting the modernization goals is the disarray in which education still finds itself. After eleven years of the domination of educational policy by the Gang of Four, a complete rebuilding was necessary. That process has barely begun.

The problems in education were recently summarized by Pu Tongxiu, deputy minister in charge of education of China's workers and staff.[2] Pu told *China Daily* that of the nation's 99 million workers (defined as factory or office personnel, as opposed to peasants), only 44 million were technical workers, of whom more than two-thirds were in grade three or below, out of a possible eight grades for workers.

The army of staff (administrative workers) totalling 20 million, is no better in terms of literacy, Pu noted. For instance, 60 to 70 percent of the 10 million staff members in industry, communications, capital construction, finance, and trades had

---

[1] *China Daily*, April 9, 1985.
[2] "Steps Taken To Improve Education for Millions," *China Daily*, March 26, 1983.

at best no more than a junior middle school (junior high) education. He said that 66 million workers and staff, or 60 percent of the total work force, were under the age of 35, of whom 30 million were junior middle school or primary school graduates.

To improve the overall level, many students were studying by TV, and Pu reported that 347,200 were in those university programs in 1982. However, the deputy minister also pointed out that many leading cadres paid little or no atention to the education of workers and that about 20-30 percent of the nation's enterprises lagged far behind and had no concrete plans for schooling their employees.

The solution, as Pu saw it, was to rotate all young and middle-aged workers into a training program. This program was implemented during 1983. The State had stipulated that every enterprise should budget an amount for worker education equal to 1.5 percent of its total wages. The State also stipulated that enterprises provide floor space for educational purposes equal to at least 0.3 to 0.5 square meter per worker. Widespread education—and consequent enlightenment—existing within the Party framework will require extraordinary efforts.

Another important part of the modernization program was to send students abroad. The Chinese were observing the hazards of such a program, with more and more of the students seeking refuge in the United States. To counteract this trend, the selection process was rigorized, resulting in sending people with "stronger ideological resolve" to the foreign study program.

Like a master of the game of chess, Deng has succeeded in surrounding, isolating, and defeating potential critics or opponents in the Politburo, especially former Vice-Chairman Wang Dongxing, once Mao's inner-Party security chief. But rumblings from Jiangxi Province, Wang's one-time bailiwick, have suggested that the purge of the Junior Gang of Four, (these last far-left leaning members of the Politburo were purged in February 1980), as they have been nicknamed, has not pleased everyone and is still controversial among some political commissars in the People's Liberation Army (PLA).

To eliminate the possibility of his own regime's being criticized and attacked in wall posters, Deng had the National People's Congress Standing Committee strike the so-called four big freedoms out of the Constitution. These freedoms, the tactical basis of Mao's Cultural Revolution, were defined as "contending, blooming (like the 100 flowers), debating, and writing posters." They are now denounced as destabilizing factors, unnecessary in view of the more conventional political rights—such as measured criticism of leaders and participation in local government elections. Every individual in a unit feels the spotlight on his daily activities. A specific time for political discussions and orientation for everyone is set aside each week. No one declines.

My interpreters became an effective sounding board for assessing how well certain of the new ideas were progressing. A case in point was Mr. Zhou, a new interpreter who replaced Mr. Ming in the early summer of 1980. He was a determined, helpful, and interested young man, intent upon learning about the airplanes, while continuing his translation duties. He exuded enthusiasm, seeming to have found a real challenge in these new technicalities. Mr. Zhou remained with us for about four months, and then we were assigned a new face—true to the policy of not allowing any one Chinese person to become too familiar with foreigners. However, through some chance, after another cycle Mr. Zhou was again assigned as an interpreter in early 1981. In the interim he had been riveted to a desk at the CAAC headquarters. He seemed genuinely elated to return to the world of real airplanes. One day I queried him about his preference.

"Mr. Zhou, which of the two assignments did you prefer?"

"What do you mean?"

"Which assignment, the desk job or the job of working more closely with the airplanes—which did you like the best?"

"Oh, I liked them both."

"Yes, I understand, but if you had a choice, which one would you choose?"

"I do whatever my unit chief assigns me."

"Of course, but you must have a preference—a personal feeling about the two jobs."

"I like them both. My unit chief decides," he shot back, his expression suggesting that the conversation was finished.

Obviously, Mr. Zhou was fearful to state a choice. Personal feelings should have no part in the serious business of job assignments. Choosing might cast a bad light on one or the other, with the hidden message that he was complaining—no attribute of a loyal worker.

The total linearity of the line of command was impressed upon me daily. The organization in which I worked, and assumed to be representative, was purely vertical. All directives and procedures came from the top. They were not to be questioned, and there was no incentive to make suggestions or to do anything differently. My interpreters would usually disappear on Friday afternoons for the political session.

On May 1, 1980, one of the most significant events in the history of the CAAC occurred.[3] On that day the all-new three-story flight kitchen near the Beijing airport opened for business. Called the Beijing Air Catering Company Ltd., it was an organization formed jointly by the CAAC and a consortium from Hong Kong, with the CAAC holding a 51 percent interest. With 4,000 square meters of floor space, and employing 250 workers and staff, including ten key people from Hong

---

[3]*China Daily,* May 1981.

Kong, the small physical size of the company belied its importance to the air fleets operating in and out of Beijing.

For the CAAC, the inauguration of reliable food service with a quality nearly matching Western sources was a giant step in the improvement of their image in the eyes of foreign travelers. However, the parsimonious nature of the Chinese once more robbed them of full benefits. Where foreign flag carriers allowed 40 yuan to be invested in each meal, the CAAC ordered a 20-yuan level on their international flights. With a capacity of 6,000 meals a day, by the end of the first year of operation the Air Catering Company was serving 2,000 meals to nine airlines, while posting an after-tax profit of 300,000 yuan.

We had planned to accept the repeated Chinese invitation to visit the Great Wall and the Ming Tombs, and the wonderful weather of May seemed like the right time. Our interpreters told us that the true measure of a man was to climb the Great Wall—leading us to believe it would be a frightfully difficult task.

The Great Wall is one of the originally designated Seven Wonders of the World, and rightly so. Rising and falling along the ridges of the Yanshan and Yinshan Mountains, which straddle northern China from east to west, the Great Wall is known as the "Ten Thousand *Li* Wall," actually stretching for 12 thousand *li* (6 thousand kilometers) from Jiayuguan Pass in Gansu Province at the west end to Shanhaiguan Pass on the shores of Bohai Bay on the east.

Construction of the Wall began in the 5th century B.C., during a period generally referred to as the Warring States Period. The cities of the central Chinese plain were frequently plundered by the nomadic tribes north of the Yinshan and Yanshan Mountains. To resist these incursions, the States of Yan, Zhao, Wei, and Qin built walls along the mountain ridges. In the 3rd century B.C., when Qin Shi Huang conquered all the other six states and became the first emperor of a unified China, he ordered his soldiers to link up all the original walls and extend them. Soldiers and peasants numbering 300,000 completed the Wall. Over the centuries, successive dynasties reinforced and renovated the Wall. In the Ming Dynasty (14th to the 17th century) major repairs were undertaken.

The Great Wall is preserved as a historical monument today, and most tourists to China take a pilgrimage to see it. The section best preserved and visited regularly is Badaling, 55 miles north of Beijing. At Badaling, the Wall is 28 feet high and 19 feet wide. Five horses or ten people can walk abreast on its crest. There are ramparts, peep-holes, and parapets, with two-storied watch towers at 325-foot intervals. There are watch towers at the top of the two ridges at Badaling, one to the east and one to the west, the highest providing a commanding view of several miles of the Wall as it fades in the distance over the undulating ridgeline.

So much was written about the Wall that it dominates the tour; nevertheless, the Ming Tombs, the other half of the day's outing, are impressive also. The Ming Dynasty, only one of the succession of feudal families who ruled the unwilling peasants of China, was an incredible period of serfdom. The Ming Dynasty survived for 276 years (1368–1644) and consumed 13 emperors, each building a magnificent tomb for his remains, projects which were begun the day each took the throne. It is said by authoritative Chinese scholars that 30,000 laborers worked for 600 years on the artifacts and the building of the tombs. Those actually involved in a certain part of the construction that revealed locations, entrances, and other vital information were cruelly killed at the end of their work so as not to leave anyone alive who could tell how to enter the tomb.

There was perhaps a very practical reason for this macabre procedure. In many of the earlier dynasties, clever grave robbers entered and pillaged the tombs. Most notable was the Tang Dynasty. Of the 18 Tang emperors buried in tombs in Shaanxi Province, 17 were plundered by a notorious grave robber named Wen Tao. In the tomb that escaped desecration, the passageway was filled with huge stones that were bolted together with iron plates. Molten iron and tin were then poured into the crevices to make a solid plug.

The Ming Tombs are located in a horseshoe-shaped valley, ringed by mountains, a classical box canyon. The valley is entered by the Sacred Way, a road beginning at a magnificent marble archway and extending four and one-half miles to the gate of the tombs. The road is lined by 24 giant-size stone statues of lions, camels, elephants, horses, and mythical animals, followed by 12 statues of generals and ministers. Each was sculpted from a single solid rock.

Of the 13 tombs, the tomb of Wan Li (Dingling) was the only one that had been opened. Behind the main pagoda that guards the tomb of Wan Li lies the large burial mound itself, 748 feet in diamter, planted with beautiful yellow pines and encircled by a massive brick wall one-half mile in length.

Initially, the burial vault was an excavation 88 feet deep. The underground tomb palace was built of marble blocks. Shaped like a "T," with a floor space of 13,000 square feet, it was built entirely without beams or columns. It is essentially a continuous series of arches, each about 18 inches wide, with meticulously fitted keystones. The height of the central hall is 23 feet. In the rear hall, the top of the "T," were the coffins of the emperor and his two empresses. Since the empresses both preceded the emperor in death, the tomb was sealed only once.

On either side of the coffins were 23 wooden chests that contained wooden figurines, women's headdresses decorated with golden phoenixes and jewels, wooden seals with the posthumous titles of the empresses, jade belts, strings of jade

Bicycles and buses form the backbone of transportation in the cities. Here in Beijing, 3.5 million bicycles are utilized by 9 million people.

Primitive practices and conditions permeate China. The widely discussed "honey wagons" proliferate, carrying human waste to the fields surrounding the cities. Air pollution is severe in the urban areas. Below, in Beijing, the estimated 3 million stoves burning high sulfur coal, nearly choked the city in the winter of 1980.

Drinking water is a scarce commodity in the large cities. Here at the entrance to Bei Hai Park in Beijing, water is being sold by the cupful. Below, to aid in pushing back the persistent drought, particularly on the North China Plain, millions of trees are being planted. Some species are given special treatment by building barriers to protect against the winter winds

T. Wilson, Chairman of the Board of the Boeing Company, presents a toast at a banquet at the Great Hall of the People on the occasion of the delivery of the first 747SP airplane to China. The most popular cuisine at Chinese banquets is the famous Peking Duck. With high demand for ducks, the Chinese have developed a force feeding technique (below), which reduces the maturation cycle from 90 to 65 days.

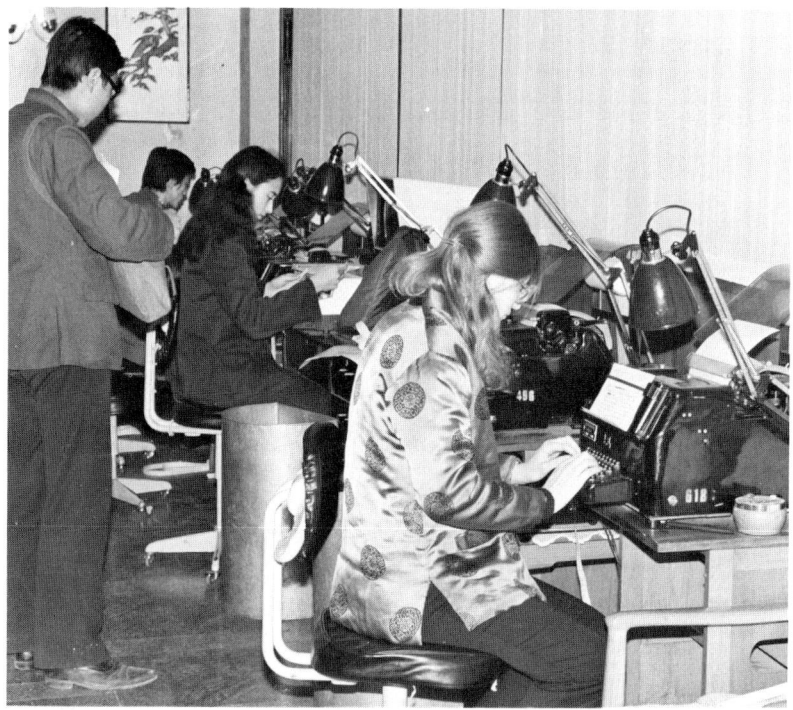

Teletype equipment was antiquated and constantly in need of repair. However, by mid-1980, new Extel and Siemens equipment began to appear. Likewise, the typewriters represented centuries-old design. The operator, using a "joy stick," manipulates the individual metal blocks to impress the characters on the platen, using carbon paper. Each tray contains 2480 characters.

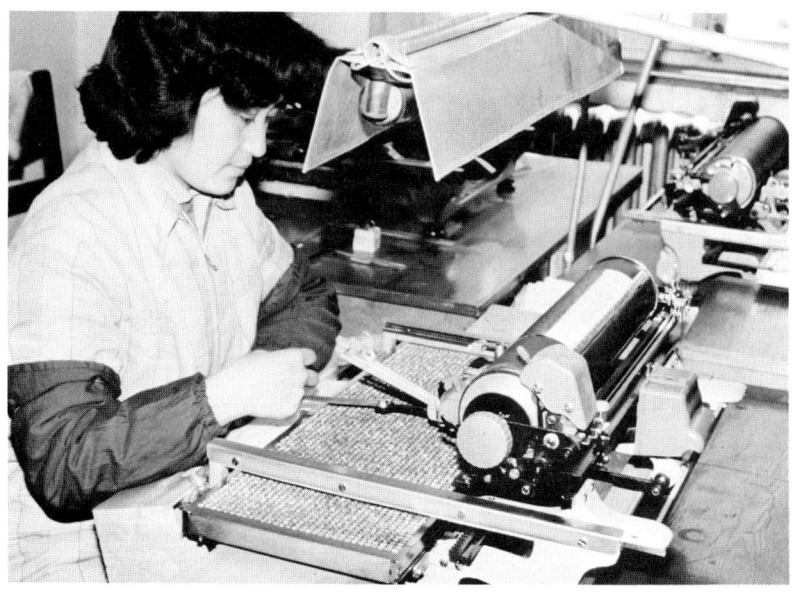

During the spring of 1981, Chinese officials became sufficiently concerned about the noise in downtown Beijing to take drastic action, forbidding the honking of automobile and bus horns in many zones of the city and imposing fines for excessive use of horns in the city at large.

Progress in local communication was given a boost in 1982, when the first sidewalk public telephone booth in the entire city of Beijing was opened.

The original maintenance building at the Beijing airport (top) was jokingly referred to as the "maintenance shack" by the Chinese, who happily adopted many American slang terms. It was stabilized with cables and concrete deadmen to avoid being blown away. The new 747 hangar (bottom), shown in a state of partial completion in September 1982, was finally opened for active use in the summer of 1984.

The people everywhere keep in good physical condition, employing Tai Jiquan, the national body exercise, practiced to a rhythmic cadence, both individually and in large groups.

Downtown Beijing had two Christian churches in 1980, one Protestant (below) and one Catholic, both quickly reaching overflowing, with crowds standing in the aisles.

January 7, 1981, witnessed an historic occasion when China opened bilateral air service with the United States for the first time in the history of the two countries. Three weeks later, on January 27, the Pan Am China Clipper appeared once again in the skies over China. The CAAC Boeing fleet was growing dramatically, with three 747SP airplanes having joined the original ten 707s.

Tibet, one of the least developed of China's five Autonomous Regions, has been selected as a prime tourist attraction. Still a nomadic society, it depends on its animal population for transportation, food, and clothing. Above, a Tibetan elder demonstrates spinning horse hair into coarse yarn for Beth Bauer and Mr. Zhou, Chinese interpreter. Below, M. T. (Mal) Stamper, Vice-Chairman of the Board of the Boeing Company, shares his supply of jelly beans with local children near Xegar, a remote Tibetan town at 14,600 elevation, near Mt. Everest.

This traditional Chinese red tractor arrived in Xegar in the decade of the 50s, first penetration of industrial equipment into this remote region. Below, in 1984, a street merchant in Xigaze, Tibet, using a modern calculator, totes up his sales. (Photo courtesy of Mal Stamper)

Seven of the Chinese mechanics who successfully completed the course at the Spartan School of Aviation in Tulsa, Oklahoma, and received their Airframe and Powerplant (A&P) licenses, pose proudly in front of the 747SP airplane. Below, the initial construction phase for the 100,000-pound-thrust engine test facility in May 1981, resulted in the completion in 1984 of a capability equal to any in the world.

Tourism in China is one of the principal sources of hard currency to fuel the modernization. The terra-cotta warriors of the tomb of Emperor Qin in Xian (commercial photo) and the Great Wall at Badaling near Beijing represent two of the most highly visited places by foreign visitors.

Almost equal to Xian and the Great Wall as tourist attractions is the Li River trip at Quilin, which many consider the most scenic place in all of China, indeed the focus of much of Chinese art. Below, the magnificent Potala Palace at Lhasa, in Tibet, is fast becoming a must visit for foreigners, as the hotel and transport facilities are gradually being increased to meet the demand.

The Jianguo, first major joint-venture hotel in Beijing, opened its doors in April 1982, creating a sensation and serving as a model for local hotel management. Below, the 1000-room, joint-venture Great Wall Hotel, one of the largest in China, and now managed by the Sheraton chain, is shown here under construction in the spring of 1983. It was opened for business in the summer of 1984.

pendants, robes, shoes, and a set of gold chopsticks, spoons, cups and washbasins. Also on the platform were wooden models of sedan chairs, coaches, spears, bows and arrows, flagstaffs with silk banners, and various other objects used in imperial processions. One of the side halls contained the coffins of the emperor's favorite concubines.

After the tomb was sealed, the earth was filled back over the construction and piled up to make the mound. The entrance was cleverly concealed, and the last of the workers killed.

In 1957, a farmer dug into a hole that appeared and found a wall containing some stones with strange inscriptions. After scholars deciphered the instructions, they determined the way to enter the main tomb. The diamond-shaped hole in the outer wall in front of the main door was pre-designed so that it could be removed, stone by stone, without collapsing the main structure. Inside were massive tandem doors, each weighing four tons, carved from a single slab of white marble. Each door was braced with a stout marble post.

Ancient artifacts were destined to contribute substantially to China's modernization efforts. As will be seen later, tourism became one of the principal sources of hard currency, and by 1981 the Ming Tombs area was attracting an annual average of 3 million tourists.

CHAPTER 8

How surprised I was on Saturday morning, May 10, 1980, to have the phone ring and hear my director's voice, calling from Tokyo. "Good morning, Gene. I called to tell you that your name is on TV all over the world!"

I groaned. The tone of his voice told me it was bad news. Then the truth dawned on me before he said another word. In my reporting routine, I had noticed that the CAAC was listing operational data on only nine 707 airplanes, while having purchased ten. One airplane was unaccounted for. I had seen a note on a previous report that airplane B-2402, the first to arrive in China, was "not in active service," a statement generally used when the airplane had been damaged or destroyed. One day I asked Mr. Yu where B-2402 was located. He peered at me curiously. "That's supposed to be some kind of secret," he laughed.

I was surprised that he would put it in those terms, having heard rumors as to the whereabouts of the airplane, most centering on the theory that the Chinese were making a copy. "Sorry I asked," I retorted. "If it is a secret, I don't want to know about it."

Now it was Mr. Yu's turn to be surprised. He could not understand why I should stop asking questions. So he continued: "Well it's in Shanghai, assigned to the Shanghai Region. They are building an airplane there."

The rumors had named the new venture the "Chinese 708,"

while the official designation was the "Yun-10" or "Y-10" for short. Hardly a day passed in the Beijing Hotel that someone did not pose a question about the Chinese copying a Boeing airplane. They wanted to know if it was true, the details, and Boeing's feeling about the program. A tantalizing latent news scoop!

With the Beijing Hotel overrun with reporters from major newspapers and magazines from all over the world, one had to be careful. I soon identified the newspeople and developed friendly relationships. However, I made it clear that I was not in China as a spokesman for Boeing, nor was my position related in any way to promotion or public relations, reiterating that my office was involved in purely technical matters. In fact, I was simply Boeing's "problem watcher" in Beijing, a phrase I had borrowed from Boeing Chairman, "T" Wilson, who always turned overzealous complimentarians away by saying his job was "chief problem watcher."

Knowing the reputation of the *Washington Post,* I was doubly careful when I talked to their reporter assigned to Beijing. A few days prior to the Tokyo call, the *Post* correspondent contacted me, saying he had a story on the 708. "I have a man who has seen the airplane in the Shanghai factory. He was invited in." He paused.

"I've heard rumors to that effect."

"Since I already have the story, I would appreciate a few facts. For example, how many 707s does the CAAC have?"

"It's common knowledge that they purchased ten airplanes in the early seventies."

"Do you know if one of those airplanes is in Shanghai?"

"I don't know anything about those activities. I think it is a Chinese secret. As a matter of fact, I am avoiding asking questions like the plague. I believe that is their business."

"What is Boeing's position on the copying of your design?"

"Frankly, I don't know what the official Boeing position

might be, but doubt that they would object. The airplane was designed in the mid-fifties and represents 20-year-old technology. But that's an unofficial opinion.''

I went on to suggest that he call the CAAC for the information he wanted, since the Shanghai region had already allowed his man into the factory. He demurred, saying he already had the story. Suspecting that he was trying to round out his release, I again told him that I was not a spokesman for the company, and what I had to say was unofficial and not for the record.

I should have offered only a "no comment," but since the reporter and I were personal acquaintances, living in the same hotel and eating in the same dining room, I felt this would be unfriendly. But he, like some other reporters in the past, took advantage of the relationship. As it turned out, he had only a weak story from Shanghai, and he used my name and position with Boeing to lend it the credence that he needed for an international news item.

The story broke in the *International Herald Tribune*. I was not only quoted, but misquoted. The big brass in Seattle had called my boss in Tokyo, inquiring, "What the hell has got into Bauer over there in China?" He said I was on the morning TV news, which came over as an official Boeing position on the "copy." From the *Tribune,* the story and versions of it came out in dozens of other newspapers.

Newsweek ran a short notice, which created another bizarre event. About a week later, the phone in my office at the airport rang; the call was long distance from Oklahoma. When I said I was Gene Bauer, the voice boomed out, "How the hell are you, old buddy?"

Stunned, I inquired who was calling. "This is Colonel Blank. Hell, you remember me. We were in Korea together. I lost contact after I returned to the States and finally retired. Then

I saw your name in *Newsweek,* and, sure as hell, you had turned up in China.''

Too incredulous to speak, I listened. Finally, I broke in to tell the Colonel that I was never in Korea and was never a colonel. ''I was honorably discharged from the United States Army in 1946 as a Staff Sergeant, after returning from duty on Okinawa,'' I told him.

The Colonel would not believe me—the reunion that he had built up in his mind was too good to blast apart. He talked on for another ten minutes, finally realizing the futility—and the expense—of continuing.

Later, when George Foster, of the *Seattle Post Intelligencer* staff, came to Beijing for a legitimate interview of a personal nature on our life in China, I was almost too shellshocked to cooperate. Nevertheless, we finally developed an understanding, and Foster turned out a good feature article as a result.[1]

As to the afteraffects of the 708 story, later in May *Aviation Week and Space Technology* interviewed John Steiner, one of the managers on the original 707 program and then a Boeing vice-president, who effectively put to rest any further speculation, indicating that the project was not to copy the 707, but was simply the result of a decade-long exercise by China to develop the capability to design and manufacture a transport aircraft.[2] I had been in the business for thirty-eight years—and was still learning.

The Chinese prototype made its first flight in September 1980, and by 1983 was flying one or two test flights per week. The Y-10 has finally been referred to by the Chinese as ''an

---

[1] ''A Busy Life for Boeing's Man in China,'' by George Foster, *Seattle Post-Intelligencer,* June 29, 1980.
[2] *Aviation Week and Space Technology,* May 19, 1980.

experimental project, not expected to lead to a production effort.''

Although the true dimensions of the Y-10 project will probably never be released for Western eyes, there is no doubt that the initial intent of the Chinese was to use the airplane as a learning base from which eventually to produce their own domestic airplanes. Reliable sources claim that over $300 million U.S., over a period of eight years, was sunk into the project in the Shanghai factory, which had been designated to do the job. If the cost was $300 million, as reported, the Chinese did not get much for their money. Two airplanes were completed and a third partially constructed, before the production concept was abandoned. One of the completed machines was a static test article. Boeing, for example, built the first commercial jet prototype, the 367-80, forerunner of the 707 line, for $16 million U.S. in the mid-fifties.

The Chinese have continually underestimated the complexity of Western tools and technology. Time and again they embark on building plants and equipment with not much more basis than visual information and an intense desire.

The Baoshan Iron and Steel complex near Shanghai was undoubtedly the most massive and most publicized effort to transplant Western technology on a large scale. With a multibillion dollar contract to the Japanese, the Chinese generally insisted on doing it their own way, even to the timing for completion, in spite of the fact that the Japanese are the recognized world's experts in steel technology. After the entire project appeared to be derailed in 1980, China first attempted to cancel the project, but reconsidered after assessing the impact on their world credibility as an industrial partner. Finally introducing some realism—and tardy planning—into the project, they reorganized to target the "first phase" completion for September 1985. Originally, contrary to advice from the Japanese, the Chinese insisted that the entire project be completed by 1982, a total of four years from construction go-ahead. To make up for a litany of foul-ups in planning the key elements, they had added an "expansion project," which will be initiated after completion of the first phase, thus extending the total program to the early 1990s.

As far back as 1910, the Chinese were pursuing Western technology. During that year, they purchased a dredge from the IHC Corporation of Holland. It was not their intent to acquire additional units, but rather to set up their own manufacturing capability. Yet in 1964 they were again buying dredges, modern counterparts of the old 1910 model. As dredge requirements proliferated, specific designs were developed for various tasks. In 1984 the Chinese were still purchasing specialized dredges, while insisting that they only wanted the technology so they could manufacture their own. They have consistently lagged in the industry by fifteen to twenty years.

The construction of the Beijing subway system eptomizes all the worst aspects of the Chinese planning methodology. In September 1984 the opening of the second link in the overall system was announced.[3] However, the link, completed thirteen years after the first construction was begun, will not be able to go anywhere near the center of the city until revisions are made which will take two more years. The ten-mile underground rail line, based on a Soviet model and finished in 1981, has been standing idle, while officials labor to get it into working order.

"It was not safe to run at that time," said Feng Shuanshen, director of the Beijing Underground Railway Administration Bureau. Equipment broke down repeatedly, a fire broke out in

---

[3] *China Daily,* September 22, 1984.

a power station, and ground water rushed in through a portion of a leaky roof.

After replacing 16 power stations, more than 600 pieces of equipment, more than 8,000 communications items, and many elevators and ventilation devices, the authorities proclaimed the system ready to go. Still, due to "technical difficulties," the new section cannot be connected to the original 15-mile line for at least another two or three years.

In aircraft, a vastly more complex technology than dredge design or subway planning, the Chinese realized they would need a fresh approach. The $300 million and seven years of effort in trying to step up to the manufacture of a 707 technology airplane was a sufficient lesson. For that outlay they could have purchased the nucleus of a modern fleet.

They were also convinced that they could not do it in even twenty years without Western technology. They decided to tie future purchases of Western airplanes to significant commitments of technology infusion and direct support of their aircraft manufacturing industry.

The Ministry of Foreign Trade, responsible for the manufacture of aircraft, first signed a contract with McDonnell Douglas in 1980 to build 100 shipsets of the DC 9-80 (later termed the MD-80 series) landing gear door in the Shanghai factory. McDonnell Douglas promised them that they would soon be co-producing airplanes. It was a heady vision.

Up to that time, Boeing had sold both the 707 and the 747 airplanes, with only modest commitments to build parts in China and to transfer technology. However, the Chinese served notice that any future purchases would require strong commitments to the modernization of their aircraft manufacturing industry.

The CAAC's need was obvious. Most of their domestic airplanes were inefficient or downright obsolete. In addition, new machines were needed to meet the rapidly expanding market.

In late 1979, Boeing Chairman, "T" Wilson, met with the machine-building arm of the Ministry of Foreign Trade, Machimpex, for preliminary cooperative discussions. By mid-1980 plans were well underway, and the traditional battle between Boeing and McDonnell Douglas was carried to China.

CHAPTER 9

By May we had developed a bad case of cabin fever in the cramped single room of the Beijing Hotel, and were ready for another attempt at breaking out.

When Frank Ching, reporter for the *Asian Wall Street Journal*,[1] described the Beijing Hotel in a December 3, 1979 article, he was expansive. At the time we were living in a rambling, ten-room rented house on Long Island, New York, and I was working in the Boeing office at the JFK airport. We had been looking forward to the trip to China and viewed Frank's article as a little bit of sunshine in an otherwise bleak report on the Chinese capital and living style.

Ching stated: "The pride of Peking's hotels is mostly for top brass and foreigners, anyway. It is home away from home for scores of Japanese and American businessmen, diplomats and foreign journalists, who live in the hotel or spend several months a year there.

"With a total of 54 banquet rooms and restaurants, the place does regular duty for State functions and private meetings of government officials with foreigners. The tourist lucky enough to snare one of the 900 rooms will find luxuries unobtainable elsewhere: airconditioning, television, and—a special touch—electric devices that open and close the curtains. "Successful foreign applicants, having been warned about primitive hotel

---

[1] *Asian Wall Street Journal*, December 3, 1979.

conditions here, are pleasantly surprised when they step into the red-carpeted interior of the Peking."[2]

Well, almost. It takes a while for the many faults of the hotel to surface. The television usually did not work, the rooms were crawling with cockroaches, and the over-friendly room boys seemed to have an excuse for being in and out of the room all day long and late into the evening.

The elevators were hilarious if one had sufficient good humor to tolerate them. The Chinese, in their own inimitable way of saving electricity, often left one bank of the twin banks of four elevators turned off, creating huge waiting queues. Maintenance was so poor that at least one of the eight would be down for repair at all times. Those working would jam, stop, fail to obey signals, and sometimes merely give up between floors. The Chinese cleaning schedule was also a mystery. They managed to be cleaning the elevators at the peak times in the morning, rendering at least an additional unit unavailable.

Nevertheless, Frank Ching had been right. The Peking Hotel was so much better than any of the other Chinese hotels, some of which had outside plumbing, requiring a clothespin on one's nose, that everyone clamored for a room. It would seem that the Chinese had not yet discovered disinfectants, instead substituting a heavy dose of perfume or burning incense, creating a unique smell which I called "perfumed urine," that signalled the location of the latrines the entire length of the corridors.

Considering the alternatives, we should have been pleased to have been settled into the "comfortable environs" of the Beijing Hotel, but after three months no one could convince us that we were having fun.

Our initial experience with the manager ruled out any fur-

---

[2] Since renamed the Beijing.

ther meetings. After that I had gone to Mr. Xu Zhengle for a bit of advice, and his only suggestion was patience. Humbug! I decided the time was right to go straight to the top, and sent a carefully phrased letter to Mr. Shen Tu, director general of the airline. In the letter I even suggested that Beth might give up and return to the United States. The only reply I received was a verbal one down through the chain of command. I was foolish to have expected more. The CAAC rarely made written replies to letters.

"Sorry," was the word. "The CAAC does not have high influence with the hotel management. They merely laugh and tell us to use our own hotel at the airport."

Dead-ended again! Reaching deep into my repertoire of approaches, I decided to try the three-martini lunch concept—only to carry it a bit further. Old as sin, bribery is cloaked under many names. *Cumshaw*, the oldest, is said to have its origin in ancient China. Called *kam sia* or *kan hsieh* (now *ganxie*), meaning "grateful thanks," both terms were used by Chinese beggars. In modern China it is called *hongbao*.

When I first approached my interpreter, Mr. Ming, with the idea of presenting a plastic desk-top model of the 747 to the hotel manager, he was aghast. He literally trembled. "Absolutely not! The Chinese would be insulted at the idea. Such bad manners! Unthinkable!" he announced.

During the days and weeks that followed, I continued to press Mr. Ming with the suggestion. I told him how inextricably the hotel business was tied to tourists, tourists to airplanes, airplanes to airlines, promotion being good for the business of all. To accept the model was simply a smart business idea—cooperation between the CAAC and the hotel was not only smart but essential. After all, the model was painted in the CAAC colors, and CAAC was already flying the first airplane—and taking delivery of two more during the summer. The black looks disappeared from his brow, but Mr. Ming feared to attempt the job. He refused to become involved.

I turned to my good friend and general fixer, Mr. Tao. He had helped me on the customs problem, and I noticed that whenever things got sticky with protocol, or a paperwork difficulty developed—in fact anything dealing with the "system"—Mr. Tao was able to have discussions with certain people, and the problems would go away. The process was known as *guanxi*. To get things done in China, one needed to have *guanxi*.

I suggested to Mr. Ming that he urge Mr. Tao to make the presentation of the model to the Beijing Hotel manager, since I was told that it would be insulting for me to do it directly. With deep misgivings, Mr. Tao agreed. To sweeten the deal, I included a few Boeing ball-point pens, calendars, and penlites. The preliminary report was hopeful. Perhaps we could get a suite in the west wing, it was suggested.

Here I must give a few more details about the Beijing Hotel. The original structure, with 100 rooms, was built by the French in 1915. In 1954 a west wing with 220 rooms was added by the Russians, and in 1974 the modern east wing was completed by the Chinese.[3] The center section could only equitably be described as atrocious and the west wing as simply ancient.

We declined the idea of a move into the west wing, reasoning that, if we accepted, the management would consider the proposition closed for all time. No, it would be better to stew in the single room until a suite opening could be achieved in the east wing. We gambled on obtaining the whole hog or nothing.

Strictly by chance, since pecking orders were rarely dis-

---

[3] *Asian Wall Street Journal*, December 3, 1979.

cernible, usually categorized as State secrets, we discovered that the assistant manager was a woman. A promising lead! I gave Mr. Tao two ladies' Shaeffer pens. That gesture added a new dimension to the negotiations, and it appeared "that a suite might become available in the east wing, but it would require a wait of a few more days." Perhaps the next turnover. Progress! Finally a breakthrough of sorts was achieved. When I inquired why it was that other foreign companies had received suites, I was told quite frankly, "They gave better souvenirs." I had been drilled on the theme that it was insulting to offer gifts of any kind, but now the truth was out. "Gift" was still a bad word—the clue was "souvenir."

The next day Mr. Tao asked whether Boeing had any small pocket calculators. Fortunately, I had one in my collection of promotion items. I also had an alarm clock, which I threw in for good measure.

Next, I received a plaintive excuse from the manager, who feared that assigning a suite to a foreign businessman would look very bad at this particular time since a drive was on to move them all out of the Beijing Hotel. However, perhaps we would be willing to move into a suite "temporarily," they suggested. We jumped at the offer. Notably, once a person was lodged, the Chinese hesitated to evict them bodily, limiting their approach to one of pleading. We were determined that, once having moved in, we would ignore all entreaties to leave.

The grand day of liberation came on June 2, 1980. Mr. Ming had gone to the hotel in the morning with the black portfolio case. Right after lunch, he called, saying he had good news. "You will be able to move into the suite tonight," he reported. Beth was ecstatic.

The suite was wonderful! Two large rooms, a large bathroom with a huge tub, a bidet, and a large set of shelves for bath notions. There was a half bath up front—and a refrigerator. The exposure was to the east, a very nice view from the 14th floor. We stayed in 1405 for the duration.

The myth of modern Chinese invulnerability to gifts had been exploded. I began to notice reports where large gifts and outright bribes with money were being accepted. So the Chinese were not basically different from everyone else, and *ganxie* survived, only with a new name.

From that day forward, the hotel staff would periodically inquire on the length of our proposed stay. We would reply that we did not know for certain, but it would be for a while longer. When I paid for the room, I would always pay for 14 days in advance. The Chinese were curious about that and tried to convince me to pay on a monthly basis, but I declined. Thus, it was inevitable that in the accounting department of the Beijing Hotel, I became known as "Mr. 14 days."

At the airport, we were preparing for delivery of the second of the three 747 airplanes. The weather had turned to full summer, clear and warm. Exactly on schedule, on June 23, 1980, B-2444 arrived to join her sister, the pioneer B-2442.

The stress of remoteness had already taken its toll of the Boeing staff. One of the three maintenance representatives had decided in mid-May that he "couldn't last a single day longer," and we let him return to the United States. I concluded that it was for the better, because the Chinese technicians were learning rapidly, and the total man-months of support that Boeing had committed would stretch further.

Our wish list of soap, Kleenex, a bicycle pump, typewriter ribbons, popcorn, and antihistamine pills was intact on the delivered airplane. On board were also several boxes of ripe, red, juicy Washington apples. The airplane was smoothly integrated into the fleet and, with no additional routes opening, provided a welcome backup to old reliable "number one."

One of the perks that the Boeing Company provided us for

accepting a permanent assignment in the remote country of China was to take a trip out each four and a half months. We were not allowed to return to the United States, but could visit the regional countries surrounding China: Japan, Thailand—and Hong Kong.

We needed those relief periods to stock up on items not available in China. However, with three 747 deliveries during 1980, we had ample opportunity to bring supplies in. Therefore, I began planning to substitute a trip to the forbidden land of Tibet. First, I had to find the means of getting there. Trains were nonexistent, and the roads were next to impassable except by six-by-six trucks. The gateway by air was Chengdu, capital of Sichuan, China's most populous province. I found that the CAAC flew to Lhasa every morning with the Illyushin 18, a four-engine turbo-prop airplane. In spite of my aversion to Russian-built equipment, we decided to seek entry.

After the PLA occupied Tibet in 1950, a treaty was signed which undermined the authority of the Dalai Lama. In 1959 Chinese troops put down an armed rebellion, killing thousands of Tibetans. The Dalai Lama fled over the Himalaya Mountains to India. In September 1965 Tibet became one of China's five autonomous regions.

Far from being a single strain, the 1.98 million people living in Tibet represent six nationalities. The region not only typifies, but magnifies, the differences that exist between the autonomous regions and the 21 provinces of China Proper. Representing only 6.7 percent of the total population, China's minority nationalities live on about 60 percent of the nation's land area.

Chairman Mao seemed intent upon either eradicating the Tibetans or forcing them into the Chinese mold. Losing their traditional culture, they had only the choice of the Chinese way of life. Most of Tibet's 6,000 or more monasteries and shrines were destroyed, sacked by mobs during the Cultural

Revolution under the slogan of abolishing the "Four Olds." Reliable sources claim that only parts of thirteen monasteries remained after the Chinese occupation.[4]

By the late seventies and early eighties the Chinese were trying to come to grips with their admitted mistakes regarding Tibet. Central to Beijing's acceptance of blame for many of the problems in Tibet was its changed view on agriculture. The Party policy had been to plant wheat, wooing or forcing the Tibetans away from their beloved *gingke* (hill barley). The staple crop, barley is ground with yak butter, tea, and salt for the traditional *zampa,* or barley cake. But the winter wheat stripped the soil of its nutrients in that high elevation, where the topsoil is thin and fragile. Yields soon dropped, reaching a point where the land failed to produce a crop. In a 180-degree reversal of policy in 1980, the Chinese began to allow barley to replace winter wheat, and by 1983 barley was again king of the highlands.

In thirty years, the Chinese had failed to bring the Tibetans into the mainstream of the Chinese nation, indeed traveling almost a full circle. The central image is not that the Chinese acted arbitrarily, although they did, bringing in mindless ideas, simply because they were common in China. The real message is that the new regime not only recognized, but was willing to admit, its mistakes, and above all to institute corrective measures.

Gradually, the Chinese attempted to heal the damage on all fronts, even tolerating Buddhist religious beliefs and promoting the return of the Tibetan language from its secondary position to the Han. By 1979 the Chinese had gained sufficient confidence in the stability of the region to begin allowing a limited number of foreigners to visit Tibet. In that year, about

---

[4]*Newsweek,* October 17, 1983: Mr. Lhasang Tsering, Central Tibetan Secretariat, Letters.

200 foreigners were admitted, all by invitation. In 1980, the first year that invitations were not required, it was estimated that 800 foreigners entered Tibet. However, specific permission was necessary for each individual.

Since I supported the airline—and planes made daily flights to Lhasa—it seemed perfectly natural that a visit could be arranged. I called Mr. Xu Zhengle for advice. He suggested that I talk to Mr. Jiang, who had established himself as our protector, guide, and general benefactor for our tours around Beijing.

Mr. Jiang was affable, kind, attentive—but firm in the belief that a visit to Lhasa at 11,800 feet elevation would be dangerous to our health. He expected that explanation to be sufficient—we would dismiss the idea. No such luck. Mr. Jiang had not reckoned with my tenacity. After several days of incubation, I brought the subject up a second time. Mr. Jiang mentioned a new hazard—strong ultraviolet radiation. The danger of overexposure to ultraviolet rays is well known. However, many thousands of people live and work their entire lives above 12,000 feet in the Himalayas of Asia and the Andes of South America with no serious ill effects—only roughening red skin on the face, neck, and hands. I laughed the problem off, and Mr. Jiang went away again.

I was beginning to wonder why the Chinese commercial airline could not easily arrange for us to go to Lhasa. My next proposal was to suggest that I would be willing to take a preliminary look at the runway there to ascertain if it was suitable for landing jet airplanes, an activity that the Chinese were anxious to promote. My suggestion fell on deaf ears. Later, I found that it was an issue in which the airline had no direct authority. Some government agency, most likely the Security Bureau, was simply dismissing the suggestion, refusing to consider the request. The Chinese leadership still did not feel comfortable about having large numbers of foreigners in Tibet.

The next road-block was the stringent physical examination required for all persons with aspirations to go to Tibet. We passed that one by offering to submit to, and pay for, all examinations that were necessary.

I was running out of ideas. My initial inquiry had been made in early May, and it was already late June. The season for visiting Lhasa was the end of March to the end of July. With a bold stroke born of desperation, I wrote a letter to the Director General of the airline, outlining the trip—on which I would accomplish a preliminary examination of the runway—and saying that I would be pleased to take one of their interpreters along, paying all flight, hotel, and meal expenses from my personal account. There was nothing but silence from the management of the CAAC.

The week before our self-imposed deadline, I made alternate plans, securing a hotel reservation in Sapporo, Japan, and completing our visa approvals. Scheduled to depart for Sapporo on the following Friday, I decided on Monday morning to call Mr. Xu Zhengle one last time.

"Good morning, Mr. Xu," I began. "I called to thank you for all the support in trying to arrange our trip to Tibet. Since it doesn't sound possible, we will be leaving for Japan the end of the week."

There was a long pause. Abruptly, Mr. Xu replied, "But, Mr. Bauer, why don't you go to Lhasa instead?"

CHAPTER **10**

OUR IMPENDING JOURNEY to Lhasa would mark our first outside trip since arriving in China. We had not yet been exposed to the ticketing, approvals, and other bureaucratic requirements of domestic travel. We decided to work the tasks one at a time, Chinese fashion. The first item was the permit for travel outside Beijing. That took two days. Actually, after we got the attention of the proper official, the procedure required only a few minutes. We filled out a form and submitted two photographs.

Next we went to the China Travel Service for reservations for lodging at Chengdu and Lhasa. No, it would have to be done by our sponsor, we were told. Besides, it was not possible to make advance lodging reservations at Lhasa. That must be done in Chengdu. We learned another basic rule about domestic travel in China: one could not get reservations for a round trip—anywhere. It was necessary to make the return reservation after arrival at one's destination.

With some trepidation, we resigned ourselves to fate. We had the uncertain promise that the travel bureau in Chengdu would secure room reservations in Lhasa, and the Chengdu CAAC office would make our return flight reservations to Beijing.

Believing the ticket purchase to be a simple transaction, on Monday morning I stopped at the central ticketing section of the CAAC on the way to the office. It proved to be far from simple. Mr. Zhou, my interpreter, spent forty minutes behind the teller's window, working with the "expert" on the Beijing-Chengdu-Lhasa route, only to discover that an error had been made in the previously announced price, forcing us to postpone the final transaction until the following morning. I suggested that the attendant proceed with making out the tickets, ready for pick-up, thus saving considerable time. "Impossible," was the reply. A ticket could not be made out unless the person was present with the money in hand.

On Tuesday the routine was repeated, again occupying forty minutes, even with the "expert" from the previous day doing the work. The experience was totally exasperating—and I had been hoping for steady progress for the CAAC—and for China.

Writing about the experience now, several years later, I must refer to my original notes to capture the despair that I felt on that day for China's modernization. As I sat in the barnlike room facing a long counter with small, teller-windowed openings in the solid plywood wall that extended to the ceiling, one for each city destination, watching the customers massed in tight groups, jockeying for position in front of the windows, everyone shouting and gesticulating, I feared with certainty that the Chinese would never break out of the cocoon that has inexorably bound them for so many centuries.

During that forlorn period of emperors and serfs, famines, floods, and wars, followed by decades of rigid monologue for quiet subservience, China—disillusioned by the Great Leap Forward, and gutted by the Cultural Revolution—had created little infrastructure, financial systems were still barely beyond barter, and social structures and behavior had stalled at the commune level.

Trapped by an intractable language, the Chinese seemed to be stuck with a grim, stoic acceptance of the unchanging and unchangeable present. Perhaps it was the destiny of China to always be so—perhaps there were places and peoples in our multifaceted world where change should not be too seriously contemplated. The programmed mediocrity of centuries would be a difficult prison from which to escape.

Looking back, I realize that my expectations had been unrealistically high. The Chinese are a happy, gentle people. Artistry is their finest talent. I was in a land not accustomed to speeding up, immersed in a people who were able to fix their vision on a far horizon and consider decades or even centuries of pits and chasms as an acceptable road to follow in reaching it.

Three years later, the domestic side of the ticketing office had not changed a single iota, except to become more congested. However, there was progress. The international side had installed computerized ticketing, and planning was going forward to begin mechanizing the domestic side. I was observing the Chinese system in action as it took each task in turn, ignoring time, with no stigma attached to postponement.

Indeed, in a major modernization announced in 1985, the CAAC revealed that a contract had been signed with the Sperry Corporation of the United States to complete a master computer system in 1986.

By the end of the week, all the details were in order, and we viewed Sunday afternoon, July 20, 1980, with anticipation for the first leg of our journey to "Shangri-la." New experiences were the order of the day. Our flight to Chengdu was aboard an IL-18, an airplane that appeared to be a Russian copy of the Lockheed Electra. The interior was thoroughly Chinese. The overhead racks were precariously piled with bags, boxes, bundles of vegetables, chickens, and assorted articles, which made up the menage of hand baggage that the Chinese tote when they travel. They invariably take their own food with them on trips, partly because service on board domestic flights is notably sparse, and partly because different kinds of food are served in the various regions of China. Local people are insistent upon their own varieties.

The 950-mile flight was reasonably smooth and uneventful, arriving in Chengdu in late afternoon. Chengdu is the traditional gateway to Tibet from China. A city of 2.5 million, the capital of Sichuan Province, which itself claims 100 million inhabitants, or fully one-tenth of all of China, Chengdu is located on a flat plain interlaced with waterways. At 29 degrees north latitude, the climate is subtropical, allowing three crops of rice to be grown each year.

After clearing the airport, and taking a taxi into the city, roughly 30 kilometers distant, we made a beeline to the CAAC offices to confirm our ongoing tickets to Lhasa the next morning, and also to secure reservations back to Beijing the following Saturday. The entire operation was surprisingly smooth.

We stayed in the 400-room Jin Jiang, the sole tourist hotel in the entire city at that time. Considering the remoteness of Chengdu and the short time that modernization had been in effect, this was not unusual. Further, other than the jumping-off place for Lhasa, an adventure not yet open to mass travel, Chengdu was not one of the mainstream Chinese tourist attractions.

The Jin Jiang boasted one section on the 5th floor with air conditioning—portable window units—and we were fortunate in acquiring a room there. The plumbing was atrocious, normal for China—not even a shower curtain—and the airconditioner labored noisily throughout the night. However, nothing short of having the place burn down would have dampened our enthusiasm—we were actually going to Lhasa in the morning.

Rising at 4:00 a.m. in order to arrive at the airport, obtain breakfast, and meet our flight, which was to leave at "sunrise," we wondered why it remained pitch-dark so long in the morning. Sunrise was not until nearly seven o'clock, a strange situation for the middle of July. The reason soon occurred to us. In China, even though the country spans five time zones, Beijing time is observed everywhere. Thus, by sun time, it was two hours earlier.

The Chinese had a very practical reason for listing "sunrise" as the Lhasa departure time. Shortly after sunrise, the ground fog rises in an impenetrable shroud, blanketing the airport for hours, sometimes until noon. Since sun time changed with the seasons, it would be foolish to specify a departure time.

After a breakfast of black coffee, roasted peanuts, and pound cake, we boarded the IL-18, standard equipment on the daily flights to Lhasa. We were airborne at 7:15, shortly after the first rays of the sun rose up over the Chengdu plain. Within a half hour out of Chengdu, we levelled off at 26,000 feet, cruising over the magnificent Hengduan Mountains, which closed around us until we were circumscribed by them.

We learned that most of the inhabitants of Tibet live in and around the valley of the Yarlung Zangbo River, a meandering glacial stream running nearly the full east and west breadth of the country. The most important tributary of the Yarlung Zangbo is the Lhasa River, with the Lhasa Valley, perhaps six miles wide in places, its jewel. Arriving over the airfield at 9:45 a.m. (7:45 a.m. sun time), we could see nothing but the many-fingered, glacial river below us. We were told that Lhasa was 65 miles distant by gravel road, a traverse of approximately two hours.

With no ground navigation facilities at the Lhasa airfield, the pilots truly flew "by the seats of their pants." I had secured permission to enter the cockpit during landing, an amazing concession by the Chinese, to take pictures of the runway as we approached. The cockpit was jammed. The Chinese flew with a five-man crew; a radioman and a navigator were added to the traditional complement of pilot, copilot, and flight engineer. The radioman and navigator are carryovers from the military; however, they are perhaps still needed in some of the remote areas where ground navigation aids are primitive. The Chinese have carried this old policy right into current operations, contracting with Boeing to provide cockpits in the 707 and 747 airplanes that would accommodate five-man crews.

As we deplaned, the station master, Mr. Da Ziyong, met us personally, having been alerted that I would be on board and would be making a preliminary examination of the runway. Our interpreter, a young Tibetan girl, was also there to meet us. Mr. Zhou could not converse in Tibetan.

As we claimed our baggage and were loading into the minibus, a sudden cloudburst exploded around us. After fifteen minutes of raging thunder and lightning, with rain driving down in torrents, the sky suddenly cleared and we were treated with the spectacularly beautiful sunshine found only at those high altitudes.

After eyeballing the runway, taking a few photographs, and recording the specifics of the construction in a discussion with Mr. Da, we climbed into the mini-bus and departed for Lhasa. As the crow flies—or in Tibet, the eagle—Lhasa is a mere 30 miles from the airfield, but by road, which winds around the bases of countless peaks following the meandering river, it is more than twice that distance. The route led us through the green fields of barley and winter wheat surrounding the communes of the Tibetans, scattered throughout the valley.

Two-wheeled wagons, pulled by nondescript teams of donkeys and horses, and loaded to the point of collapse, congested the narrow, gravel roadway. Tibetan women, bending under huge loads of brush gleaned from a morning's labor on the mountain slopes, were returning to their communes.

After two hours of bumping along the rough road, dodging donkeys, cattle, pigs, and chickens, as well as human traffic, we caught sight of the golden-towered Potala Palace, thrusting up from the valley floor of the Lhasa River. As we drew closer, the low-profiled city, sprawling along the river, came into view. The fields on the outskirts were abundant with vegetables, and the barley and winter wheat were fast maturing in the brilliant sun.

We were taken to the 80-bed Gong Pa Sha guest house on the outskirts of Lhasa, the only hostelry available to foreigners at the time. The accommodations were far better than we had dared hope. Each unit, a duplex of concrete block construction with a tiled roof, contained a double living room, bedroom, and bath. Electricity and hot water were included in the amenities.

We immediately noticed and appreciated the crisp mountain air, a rewarding environment to the traveler from polluted Beijing. The temperature too was a pleasant surprise. The 29-degree north latitude provides a perfect balance to the high elevation in ameliorating the climate to produce an equitable summertime temperature of 65 degrees F.

We had come unprepared to witness such a curious, hospitable people. Foreigners were almost as rare in Tibet as the whooping crane was in the United States, and the natives were intent on scrutinizing every one of us. Merely to appear on the street in a mini-bus was to have everyone stop and stare. There were perhaps less than a dozen such vehicles in the city of 120,000 inhabitants, and we saw only one automobile during the entire visit. To walk down the street meant to be engulfed in a surging crowd. I instinctively protected my pockets and wristwatch, but there was no need for alarm. The people were scrupulously honest. Their interest was pure childlike curiosity.

Outside Lhasa, the Tibetans lived in communes similar to those in China, except much smaller, or traveled as families with their animals, following them with the seasons. They were a closely knit people, wards of a capricious natural environment, sharing both scarcity and abundance.

From the time the rulers of Tibet killed people as sacrifices, even burying children alive in the cornerstones of their new temples, the Tibetans have made great progress. An agrarian, simple folk, they were open, friendly, and cooperative, uncomplaining and hard-working, happy with the small pleasures of an uncomplicated existence. Nowhere could one find a people with more expressive faces, more piercing eyes, more inquisitive manners.

With the help of the Chinese, Lhasa was slowly building a rudimentary industry. A carpet factory thrived where feminine artisans worked with dexterous hands to fashion the most beautiful and sought-after carpets in the world. On the outskirts, a cement plant was in operation, and two small hydroelectric facilities provided power for the city and a growing portion of the countryside.

We were invited to tour the Ma (Horse) commune, a community of 500 people up the valley southwest of Lhasa, and we spent almost a full day enjoying the experience, hardly noticing the altitude. The commune revealed the sharp contrasts between the ancient and the modern. Rooted in centuries of a vaguely recorded past, the people were slowly absorbing the nuances of Western culture. Electric lights were beginning to penetrate the darkness of their bedrooms; an occasional alarm clock and even a radio could be seen; yet just outside the door of the house of stone, mud, and sticks a newly mothered sow suckled her one-week old piglets, and chickens roamed freely in the yards.

Buddhism still holds a central thread in the lives of the Tibetans. They visit the Potala Palace to pray and to make offerings. Built in the 7th century, gutted by fire in the 8th, and rebuilt in the 17th by the fifth Dalai Lama, the palace is an architectural marvel, considering the materials and methods of construction available at the time. A massive edifice of wood and stone, the 13-storied palace sweeps up from the southern slope of Potala Hill to its summit, soaring more than 358 feet above the street and measuring over 1,170 feet from east to west.

In spite of desire and effort, the great palace is yielding to the forces of weather, mold, and decay, as a small reconstruction force works in vain to maintain it. Gone are the days when 7,000 slaves could be marshalled at the snap of a finger to labor with no reward but a bare existence.

Old Lhasa is a menage of narrow streets, crumbling wood and stone buildings, tents of herdsmen and farmers. Cattle, goats, yaks, pigs, and chickens wander at will among the sidewalk vendors who spread their wares on tattered rugs or blankets on the ground.

We spent four days in the ancient splendor of Lhasa, and will not soon forget those magnificent mountains and the simple, patient people.

Shortly after we departed, a group of Western news reporters arrived in Lhasa by invitation of the government. Coincidentally, the brother of the exiled Dalai Lama, a professor at the University of Indiana, was also there at the time. Seeing the brother of their revered, exiled leader, the townspeople erupted in a spontaneous demonstration, in full view of the contingent of news-hungry correspondents. Soon after that incident, the restrictions for visitors tightened again, and very few foreigners were allowed to visit Lhasa during the next three years.

However, the Chinese continued to show the pragmatism that pervades the new regime. Encouraged by their own progress in improving Tibetan economic conditions, they began preparing for a larger influx of foreigners. In December 1983 the old IL-18 airplanes were retired from the Chengdu-Lhasa run, replaced by 707 jets, which by the spring of 1984 were making ten flights per week. Ground was also broken for the Tibet Hotel, a new, modern hostelry for tourists.[1]

In the fall of 1984, the Chinese announced that tourists were again welcome in Tibet.[2] All they needed was a hotel room and a pocketful of cash. The ambitious plan for tourism visualizes 6,000 visitors in 1986, growing to 100,000 a year by the turn of the century. To accommodate this influx, ten new hotels were under construction in Tibet in mid-1985, four of them in Lhasa.[3]

A whole host of other actions were also promised, including development of hydroelectric power, establishment of a local airline, government support of local handicrafts, promotion of commerce with other provinces, and the training of 10,000 Tibetan intellectuals by the end of this decade.[4]

Thus, the modernization drive was already making itself felt in the outer reaches of the Chinese nation five years after it was declared. Indeed, the Chinese appeared determined to make a showcase of Tibet for all the world to see, while extracting the flood of tourist dollars that are certain to come.

[1] *China Daily,* May 15, 1984.
[2] *Ibid.,* October 6, 1984.
[3] *Ibid.* June 22, 1985.
[4] *Ibid.,* July 24, 1984.

CHAPTER 11

DELIVERY OF the third 747 airplane ordered by the CAAC was imminent when we returned from Lhasa, but problems in financing had developed as a result of stalled bilateral negotiations for air service between the United States and China. The Chinese had originally intended to pay cash for the three airplanes, as they had done on the 707 purchase nine years earlier.

During the negotiations, it was realized that flights to the United States created the possibility for a leveraged lease. Responding to favorable terms provided by the U.S. tax laws, Lazard Freres and Company arranged a lease with Manufacturers Hanover Leasing Corporation, who became the owner and trustee, under a $51 million, 15-year agreement. By the lease, U.S. tax benefits accrued to Manufacturers Hanover, and a preferred interest rate was available to the Chinese.[1]

The leasing arrangement was a landmark in Chinese financial innovations in dealing for foreign industrial goods, a drastic departure from the old "cash-on-the-barrelhead" philosophy. However, the Chinese soon discovered that leasing also brought unforseen obligations. They were no longer allowed to register the airplane in their own country: U.S. registry was mandatory, bringing with it the full weight of the FAA regu-

---

[1] *Aviation Week and Space Technology,* December 15, 1980.

lations for its operation. Thus, the Chinese were obliged to contract for additional maintenance support, finally choosing Pan American. Under the FAA rules, a mechanic with a U.S. Airframe and Powerplant (A&P) license was required to approve work done by the CAAC mechanics and to sign off the airplane on every departure from a Chinese airport.

My initial instructions to the Boeing maintenance support team had been, "Work yourselves out of a job as soon as possible." A literal charge, it was intended to force the Chinese to step up to new problems and become independent. Although slowly and painfully, the strategy worked.

The Chinese had continued to postpone the critical task of engine buildup for their first spare engine. It was originally planned for the end of May, but unforeseen handling problems due to lack of proper equipment caused a number of delays. Thus it was not until the middle of August that they were ready for the specialist from Rohr Aircraft Company, builder of the nacelle assembly, to come to Beijing to supervise and to teach the Chinese to do the job.

Ever since the first airplane arrived the previous February, the CAAC had blithely ignored the need for a spare engine, unconcerned that they were badly exposed in operating two aircraft—eight engines—with no backup for emergency. In the event that one of the operating engines ingested a bird or other foreign object, the airplane could have been grounded until a replacement engine was acquired, probably leased by the month at an exorbitant fee.

Whenever I discussed the urgency of engine buildup during the spring and summer, the Chinese laughed off my concern with the remark, "Oh, the airplanes are new; nothing can go wrong." Consisting of installing the accessories, electrical harness, hydraulic tubing, nose cowl, thrust reversers, and tail cone, engine buildup represented not only a considerable number of man hours but also highly technical skills. Even a well-trained crew would require a full day. Since it was a first effort, the Chinese took three weeks.

After the bare engine was removed from its sealed, silica gel–protected container and mounted on the engine buck, the Chinese inspected it for shipping damage. During inspection, an incident developed about which I joked with John Hertel, the P/W representative, as "Beware of a man in a straw hat." John and I had gone to the engine shop to observe and assist. There, standing on the rail of the buck, was a peasantlike man in a straw hat, wearing the typical monochromatic garb of trousers and tunic. His mission was to examine the engine for acceptance. After a cursory inspection, he grandly announced, "This is not a new engine!" Pointing to the straw and blue tones on the metal walls of the turbine hot section, he complained that these were signs that the engine had been used.

Every new engine undergoes a "green run" in the test cell, to check its operating parameters and to assure that everything is within specifications. The engine is in fact "used" from that day forward. However, these run-in tests last no more than a few hours. Our man in the straw hat had initially impressed the unknowing CAAC mechanics gathered around, and they quickly turned questioning glances toward John Hertel, who had a difficult time holding his temper.

It did not help the situation when, at the moment that John moved in to explain via our interpreter, Mr. Straw Hat stepped on the oil tank, squarely on top of the sign in one-inch high letters which said "NO STEP." Furious, John began flailing at his ankles with his steno pad, yelling for him to get off. Confused, Mr. Straw Hat stepped off immediately, planting his free foot and full weight on an engine breather tube, which was attached with a brazed joint and easily damaged.

By this time the assembled CAAC mechanics began to doubt the expertise of their "expert." Inquiring who he was, we were told he was a retired engineering executive now on the advisory staff, who in the old days had extensive responsibility for engines. Perhaps he was a throwback to the reciprocating engine and propeller days, or even a Party leader who had been masquerading as an expert when dedication to doctrine was much more valuable than knowledge. In any case, he stepped down, disappeared, and was never seen in the engine shop again.

That incident increased our wariness concerning the handling of sophisticated equipment and reinforced my conviction that the Chinese had a tremendous gap to overcome before they would be fully capable of understanding the 747 airplanes.

The delivery of airplane number three was postponed during the financial negotiations; it finally arrived on the 21st of September. If the delivery was a test of China's infrastructure, the Chinese failed the test. On Tuesday, September 23, 1980, the airplane was ready for formal delivery. To handle all the formalities caused by the lease deal, a four-way telephone call had been pre-arranged among Beijing, New York, Seattle, and Oklahoma City. All the principals, using a pre-written script, were to go through the delivery details, culminating in legally transferring the airplane to the CAAC, who had set the meeting up in a large conference room in the newly built airport hotel. The Boeing people began looking for telephones and soon discovered there was not a single phone in the room, nor any provisions for jacking them in. The meeting was quickly adjourned to another location.

Availability of the airplane for revenue service proved to be not a day too soon. The very next day, the unusual string of luck in operating without a spare engine ran out. Operational errors during landing resulted in overheating of one of the engines. The exhaust gas temperature (EGT) indicator pegged out at 1,100 degrees C., considerably beyond the maximum allowable temperature. The airplane was ferried (non-passenger flight) on three engines back to Beijing for an engine change. The newly delivered airplane was immediately pressed into service. The engine change took four days, a long time even for a first effort. The Chinese had a target to shoot for: Pan Am's best time was one hour and fifty minutes.

With no capability for engine repair in China, it was imperative to ship the damaged engine to the United States. Shipping a five-ton engine halfway around the world is no small task. Early in the 747 program, anticipating such requirements, Boeing had developed a "fifth pod" kit, which allows a spare engine to be slung beneath the left wing, between the fuselage and the number two position. The fifth pod engine merely goes along for the ride, but its carriage has been certified with the FAA, and it is permitted on regular passenger flights.

However, the CAAC had not yet uncrated their fifth pod kit, nor had they translated the instructions for mounting and carrying it, exposing again the aggravating Chinese trait of linear thinking. In spite of my urging to activate the kit, the Chinese chose to weigh other possibilities, of which there were two: ship by surface transportation or pay air freight charges to another airline for carriage on the main deck of a 747 cargo airplane.

With the cost of air freight coming to $52,000, and the cost of ocean freight $8,000, the choice of shipment by sea was a foregone conclusion. No consideration was given to the fact that a $4 million spare asset would be unavailable for a long period of time.

The engine was recrated in its original container, sent by special truck to the seaport at Tianjin, by sea to Hong Kong for reloading on a larger ship, then again by sea to the east coast of the United States via the Panama Canal.

Even though Pratt/Whitney required less than thirty days for inspection and repair, the engine did not arrive back in Beijing until thirteen months later, in November 1981.

In most airlines of the world, such a series of events would have triggered a crash "get well program" aimed at activating their fifth pod kit. Typically for the Chinese, nothing was done. The immediate need had gone away. In fact, the following February, when another engine required removal in New York, the fifth pod kit had not yet been activated. Further, the CAAC had refused to leave the first repaired engine in the United States as a rotatable spare and were forced to lease an engine from Pan Am. Central control was all-important in the Chinese mode of operation. It had been decided that all spares must remain in Beijing.

At Beijing, the fifth pod kit was still uncrated, and the operational instructions remained untranslated. This continued lack of attention to future planning forced the Chinese to contract with Pan Am to ship the leased engine back to the U.S., using a Pan Am fifth pod kit. Pan Am mechanics came from Tokyo with the kit, built it up, installed it on their own airplane, and flew the leased engine back to New York—at considerable expense to the CAAC.

This series of events involving engines is cited as a typical malaise in the planning process of most Chinese industrial and commercial concerns. The linear planning technique, useful for centuries in old China, was proving to be woefully inadequate as a tool for meeting modern business demands.

September was not all bad news, however. The new airplane, N1304E, performed well and the schedules were met.

With the harvest approaching, we were taken on a tour of a large commune near Beijing. Essentially a dairy with 1,700 Holstein cows, the commune of 32,000 people in 8,000 families also produced ducks, pigs, chickens, eggs, corn, wheat, rice, castor beans, pears, apples, peaches, and grapes.

The white Peking ducks are hatched in incubators, and put immediately on a feeding cycle of sixty-five days. The last twenty days are devoted to force-feeding. The ducks are shooed into a funnel-shaped enclosure that has at its terminus a single narrow chute. As each duck pops out, heading for supposed freedom, a peasant woman firmly grasps it by the neck, and in a series of deft motions opens its bill by pressing on the sides of its cheeks, rams the duck's head onto a half-inch diameter plastic tube that protrudes from the mixing machine, steps on a treadle that spits out a measured slug of rich cereal mash directly into the duck's crop, and reaches for the next "victim."

The "zapped" duck dashes for the exit, wobbling from disorientation and top-heavy as a result of the huge lump in its throat. For the next four hours, the force-fed ducks are content to squat in the sunlit yards or in their pens, in a half-stupor while the food is being ground up in their gizzards. Force-feeding continues four times a day for the full twenty days, when the ducks are ready for market. The technique reduces the maturation cycle by nearly one-third.

The brisk, bright month of October, historically the finest month in Beijing, was a joy, the last before the freeze of winter, which would begin during the first week of November.

In Beijing, at 40 degrees north latitude and inland sufficiently to miss an amelioration of climate from the ocean, autumn is a two- to three-week interlude between summer and winter.

In the operation of the 747 airplanes, I was continually confronted with frustrating events which focused on the paucity of communication among the Chinese at all levels, and their seeming incapability for innovation. A particular instance involved the third airplane. Mr. Xu Zhengle had gone to Tokyo to negotiate with Pan Am for a maintenance contract. A semi-emergency had developed, which required that I contact him. Calling the CAAC headquarters, my interpreter was told that no one knew which hotel he was staying in. Unbelieving, I asked him to inquire who in the booking office had made his airline reservation. No one knew that either. After calling several more people in headquarters, the interpreter gave up, saying it was impossible.

Deciding to try myself, I called Mr. Xu's office. Fortunately, I was connected with someone who spoke English. Posing the same questions, I received the same responses, but, continuing to probe from different angles, I was able to make suggestions to explore other avenues. Finally, I learned that the hotel reservations had been made by the Chinese Embassy in Tokyo. That made it easy. I contacted the Boeing office in Tokyo, and was speaking to Mr. Xu within the hour.

I had accomplished with one call what my interpreter had failed to do in thirty minutes with multiple calls, speaking in his native language. The Chinese are too willing to accept *meiyou* (don't have, or can't do) for an answer, even regarding an unanswered telephone as sufficient reason to give up. Content to react to events, they are not willing to try "to make things happen."

Another major impediment to progress continued to be the difficulty of translation of technical terms into Chinese characters, and their subsequent processing through the primitive Chinese typewriters. In some ways the typewriter resembles a printing press, with its large 9-inch by 20-inch horizontally placed platen containing 2,480 characters, each inscribed on a small metal block. The operator, using a joystick, picks up each character individually, moves it up to the 4-inch-diameter, 20-inch-wide roller, and impresses the character to the page via a carbon paper overlay. Extremely skilled operators can transfer no more than 50 characters per minute, while the average well-trained typist can do about 30 per minute. To provide for extra flexibility, two auxiliary trays are available, each with 1,000 characters. These 4,480 characters are sufficient for most non-technical writing. However, technical writing is still very specialized. An additional 5,000 characters are available for such endeavors.

Once translated, the material was used by the mechanics only when everything else failed. They would rather grab their toolboxes and make a beeline for the airplane, using trial-and-error, feel-and-sight techniques, constantly being forced back reluctantly to read the recommended procedures. When they did finally begin to use the translated maintenance manuals, they often removed the pages, taking them to the airplane, occasionally soiling, tearing, or losing them.

In spite of all the trials and obstacles, the Boeing-CAAC relationship continued to grow and flourish. Related activities with the Chinese aircraft manufacturing complex also began to show progress.

Foreign aircraft sales agreements are laced with side letters providing training credits, spare parts credits, computer software, and other benefits that lower the cost to the airline. One of the most cherished of these concessions is the "offset" work that represents manufacturing of parts and assemblies in the airframe factories of the host countries.

China, chastened by its extravagant venture with the Yun-10 and with little to show for their investment of $300 million, was intensely pursuing a major manufacturing program with one of the main U.S. producers of commercial airplanes, namely; Boeing, Lockheed, or McDonnell Douglas.

Lockheed was never seriously in contention. The ill-fated Tristar had already reached a zero new-sales level, and the corporation had decided to phase out their commercial aircraft business.

McDonnell Douglas, pushing a rosy-hued scenario, which the Chinese initially accepted on faith, established the first beachhead, even though they had yet to sell an airplane to the Chinese. They were off the starting blocks as early as 1979, looking to a decision for an ambitious program for a joint-venture production effort. McDonnell Douglas expected to have the Shanghai Aircraft Factory, which would start by making landing gear doors for the DC 9-80, ready for major assemblies and even a complete production line by mid-decade.

Early in 1980, the Chinese had backed off on the joint-venture go-ahead, but nevertheless, signed a contract for assembly of 100 shipsets of the DC-9 landing gear door. To be completed within three years, with the promise of 100 additional shipsets, the contract value was around $1 million, and would run to 1985. McDonnell Douglas provided the raw materials, since the Chinese metals, alloys, and non-metallic materials were not qualified for use in FAA certified airplanes. However, of the 350 tools and fixtures required for manufacturing the parts and assembling the doors, most were fabricated in the Shanghai factory, where McDonnell Douglas assigned tooling and quality control engineers to provide direct support.

The first completed door assembly was delivered to McDonnell Douglas in January 1981. Although the door program was successful in itself, it quickly became clear that the basic knowledge, machine tools, measuring devices, plant capacity, and managerial talents were totally inadequate for a joint venture of the scale contemplated in the decade of the eighties, without massive foreign technology infusion and direct support.

McDonnell Douglas had initially overestimated the Chinese

technological, manufacturing, and management capabilities. The Chinese, fully aware of their own deficiencies, postponed the decision to start a production program.

In the meantime, Boeing was exploring a different approach that would utilize still another Chinese aircraft factory, the Xian facility. The Boeing plan was essentially a step-by-step operation, beginning at the most fundamental levels—machining simple parts and training engineers in aircraft design, tooling, production, and quality control.

The Boeing effort was officially kicked off in the fall of 1979, when Chairman "T" Wilson met with officials of Machimpex, the agency responsible for machine building. Wilson's statement was pragmatic and purposeful: "Boeing will assist China in its modernization efforts, and will offer the kind of assistance and cooperation to meet China's national interest and industry capability requirements on a mutually beneficial basis."

In September 1980 the first round of working discussions was completed, leading to a many-faceted program, configured in a non-time-dimensional series.

The first contract included the training of fifteen Chinese engineers in the Boeing plants in Seattle, Washington. The engineers were selected from a list of graduates of Chinese universities, a selection based on their English language ability and their orientation to specific fields. The chosen fields were propulsion, aeronautics, flight controls, structures, systems, quality control, and research and development.

The second leg of the Boeing cooperative program with China provided for the production of aircraft hardware and included manufacturing know-how, quality control, facilities acquisition, and management planning and control. The first phase was a parts machining program consisting of the production of Model 737/747 detail parts, with Boeing providing the raw materials. Total pieces in the $1.2 million program were 4,960, representing 106 different part numbers. The second phase added minor assemblies, the third phase more complex assemblies, the fourth phase a complete section, and, finally, with no stated time frame, the capability to produce a complete aircraft.

In anticipation of the day when the Chinese would need their own fully qualified raw material sources and specifications for control, a third leg was included in the program, that of qualifying forging processes and, finally, forgings themselves.

The total program was based on a crawl-before-you-walk, walk-before-you-fly, philosophy, which found immediate acceptance at the levels where pragmatism is prevalent: the design rooms and the factory floor. However, there were still those in the higher echelons who clung to the myth of a Great Leap to proficiency.

In December 1980 the initial contract was signed between Boeing and China National Aero-Technology Import and Export Corporation (CATIC), a trading corporation in aircraft manufacturing. With McDonnell Douglas proposing to do the complete job in an incredibly short time, all the elements of a full-scale, no-holds-barred sales competition for the next level of need, a medium-range airplane for the Chinese domestic market, were on the table.

CHAPTER 12

Lack of innovation in the Chinese was not simply an analytical weakness, but a deep-seated manifestation of centuries-old attitudes and outlooks. In October 1980 an event on the flight line again reinforced that certainty.

When an auxiliary power unit (APU) on one of the 747 airplanes failed to start, the Chinese mechanics completed the prescribed trouble-shooting procedures. At least so they said. When the unit continued to malfunction, they came to the Boeing office for assistance. The Boeing technician quickly diagnosed the most probable cause, an explanation which the Chinese immediately rejected, saying they had already checked that possibility.

The part in question was a high-pressure metal filter in the APU line. With the symptoms of fuel starvation, the filter was the prime suspect. Naturally we were obliged to take the Chinese mechanics' word that they had checked the filter, and assumed that they had read the maintenance manual and performed the recommended tests. Thus we proceeded to search for other causes—in vain.

A full day passed, with the airplane out of service, when we decided to request assistance from our central engineering support group at the home plant. Their advice was the same as we had previously given—change the high-pressure filter. At that juncture, the Chinese willingly complied, and the problem disappeared.

We were disappointed and angry, reminding the Chinese of the instructions in the manual to perform a specific pressure differential test to determine the flow characteristics of the filter. Upon further quizzing, they admitted that they had made only a visual check.

It was apparent that because of non-technical backgrounds, most of the mechanics took an oversimplified view of complex equipment. Their reluctance to read instructions, preferring to rely on their own sense of sight and touch, was proving to be their most enduring trait, and a major impediment to progress.

I began to suspect more and more that the Chinese were, on occasion, lying to me, and eventually situations developed where I felt certain of it. My suspicions were reinforced when I read of the experiences of a Special Magistrate in Hong Kong in 1949.[1] The Magistrate was discussing the use of oaths in courtroom procedures. He stated: "Naturally, in a Chinese court, no one is expected to tell the truth, and few ever do. Perjury is a word all but untranslatable into Chinese. In every suit it could be confidently assumed that everyone would tell lies. It was the magistrate's duty to sift the lies."

The Magistrate went on to say: "As a senior Chinese colleague of mine in the Hong Kong administration, for many years a Magistrate himself, once wisely said to me, 'No Chinese is going to tell the truth unless he can see some advantage in doing so. Why should he? *Truth is private property.*' "

The largest industrial exhibition ever held by the United States in China, sponsored by the U.S. Department of Commerce and including exhibits from 250 domestic firms, was presented in Beijing during the period of November 15 to 28, 1980. Officially named the U.S. National Economic and Trade Exhibition, the exhibition was to provide Chinese industrial

[1] *Myself a Mandarin, Memoirs of a Special Magistrate,* by Austin Coates. Heinemann Asia, 1968.

personnel a first-hand opportunity to view equipment representing many fields of advanced technology.

The campaign to sell the 737 airplane to the Chinese for their domestic system was well underway, and Boeing used the occasion of the exhibit to emphasize the advantage of that airplane and the attributes of the rest of their jet family.

McDonnell Douglas was there too, showing a nearly completed landing gear door from the Shanghai Aircraft Factory. In December I reduced the Boeing contingent another notch, to one man in addition to myself, and with that level we completed the contracted thirty-four man-months of technician support at the end of 1981. I could begin to see progress in the capability of the Chinese technicians, even though they followed a serrated learning curve—advancing three steps and falling back two.

In mid-November, the CAAC had added 747 service to London via Sharjah and Frankfurt on a one flight per week cycle. My friend and general fixer, Mr. Tao, was assigned as the deputy manager of the London office. He went on single status, allowed to return only once a year for two weeks to visit his family. Family separation was not unusual in China. It was the way of life. In many instances, husband and wife worked in different provinces and were separated for a year or more at a time, all their working lives. Permission to travel was required in advance and conveyed only from a high level of authority.

With the 747 gradually moving toward the position of maturity in the CAAC operations, I began to look at some of the support considerations within the CAAC organization. To my dismay, I discovered the non-existence of a separate quality assurance group. The mechanics, after completing a task, would simply report that fact to their group leader.

After reviewing several instances of equipment and system malfunction in the 707 fleet, and tracing them to poor follow-up, the CAAC created a quality-control organization, the first since the airline was founded. No other single event was more significant to the eventual success of the airline in achieving its goal of recognition as a first-rate international entity, with an FAA approved repair certificate. They had taken a first painful step in introducing checks and balances into their rigid system.

Another aspect of the CAAC organization, which was choking progress to a trickle, was internal communication. In addition to the reticence about individual communication on a lateral basis, the procedure for handling messages was still in the dark ages. Letters from the Beijing Region, only 30 kilometers from downtown headquarters, often took seven days for transit. I found that copies of telexes and other correspondence that I routed to headquarters from my office were sometimes never delivered.

In late November, Beth and I prepared to depart for our first "rest and recuperation" trip out of China. We planned a one-week trip to Hong Kong to enjoy Western food and to purchase the items on our growing "wish list."

Again, we flew on a CAAC 707, the cabin service now worlds improved over the flight on which we came to China. The food was good, a tribute to the new Hong Kong Catering Service in Beijing that was scarcely six months old.

We never realized how confining and bare an existence we had been enduring until we arrived in Hong Kong. We stocked up on many small and common items not yet available in Beijing: razor blades, toothpaste, cough drops, pantyhose, shaving soap, manila envelopes, scotch tape, rubber bands, cold pills, small batteries, deodorant, typewriter ribbons, iodized salt, baking soda, and toothbrushes. We had our teeth cleaned and ordered new eyeglasses. Dentistry is primitive in China and available only to a very few. The 800 million peasants rarely, if ever, visit a dentist.

We swam in the hotel pool, a joy after one despairing dip in the International Club pool in Beijing, which was so badly polluted that people broke out in rashes and even became seriously ill. Best of all, we escaped the fierce, dirty Beijing winter for a full week.

Shortly after we returned to Beijing, Christmas was upon us. The Chinese do not recognize Christmas, but nevertheless celebrate it in some circles in deference to the foreign community, generally lumping it together with New Year's Day.

On Christmas Eve we enjoyed three separate parties. To start, we were invited to a fabulous buffet at Ambassador Leonard Woodcock's residence, first Ambassador to China and a U.S. "lame duck" in a losing election year. The Embassy children presented a Christmas pageant, and a group of talented adults sang carols. We departed early to attend a special reception hosted by the CAAC as a "New Year's Party" in the Hubei Room of the Great Hall of the People.

The Great Hall, a massive structure of stone and marble, has a volume of 56,000,000 cubic feet and is one of the world's largest buildings. The grand assembly auditorium alone, where the National Congresses convene, covers over an acre and seats 10,000 people. There are 29 huge meeting rooms, one for each of the 21 provinces, 5 autonomous regions, and 3 municipalities, furnished in the local style and with local handicrafts. The Chinese claim to have built the gargantuan edifice in ten months, a claim doubted by everyone who has ever entered its doors, but proved to be incorrect by none.

The Hubei Room was laid out with two long tables, heavy-laden with food. The Chinese presented singers, dancers, and musicians for entertainment, and also suggested some do-it-yourself additions. The Japan Airlines representative sang two Chinese songs, the Pakistani representative sang an Indian song, and the North Korean sang two Korean songs. Recognizing that the invitation was more like a request, and after some coaxing, Beth, a professional singer, and John Hertel, with a strong voice, joined to sing the "Star Spangled Banner"—a real "believe-it-or-not" happening which indicated how far the Chinese had come in their thinking.

Following that event, which ended promptly at 9:00, we returned to the Grand Ballroom of the Beijing Hotel to watch the Chinese acrobats and magicians, and to dance to some recorded Western music. The Chinese had taken a particular liking to "Jingle Bells" and played it over and over. Beth was asked to dance with a Chinese Santa Claus. He could not dance, but was trying to learn.

The autumn of 1980 brought additional manifestations of the Chinese modernization program. A personal income tax law was passed, to take effect in October. The law required all foreigners to register prior to the end of the year.

Further, we were told to pay our October and November taxes before the end of December. The law was patterned after the U.S. income tax laws, with a graduated schedule. The zero tax level, at an income of 800 yuan ($475 U.S. at the time) per month or less, was sufficiently high to exempt 99 percent of the Chinese, if not all. It was purely a tax on foreigners—another method to get hard currency into the Chinese coffers quickly.

As evidence of earnings, I requested Boeing to send me a notarized statement at the end of each month. With a ten-day-minimum one-way mail transit time, I expected to receive them by the 15th of the month. Appearing at the tax office on the 30th of December, I declined to pay any tax, requesting a stay until the 15th of January. The tax authorities pointed to the law, which stated that a fine could be imposed for payment after the 7th of the month, for the previous month's tax. I explained the problem with the mail.

"Why can't Boeing send the statement early?" they inquired. I emphasized that sometimes the pay day came on the last day of the month, since I was paid on every other Thursday. "Oh, then you should pay an estimated tax and settle the plus or minus differences the next month," they concluded. I continued to decline, repeating that I would pay prior to the 15th. Finally, the Chinese agreed and everything worked out well for the next few months, with my statements arriving well in advance of the deadline.

One day my letter from Boeing arrived on the 14th of the month. When I appeared at the tax office, I was greeted by a new group of collectors. They reviewed the law. "Since you are late, you could be fined," they announced, "but we will do you the favor of not imposing a penalty in this instance."

Bridling, I stormed: "Please do not do me any favors! I have an agreement to pay by the 15th, and I respectfully decline to pay any fines whatsoever for late payment at any time in the future."

"You will be forcing us to break the law," they retorted.

I turned to my interpreter. "Please inquire how many days I must spend in jail for late payment, since I decline to pay any fines."

The interpreter turned ashen. Incredulous, he stared at me. "I cannot ask them that; they are authorities," he protested.

I insisted, repeating the request several more times. Reluctantly, he complied. After an embarrassed discussion, the tax people announced the the 15th would be perfectly satisfactory. They were all smiles. I experienced non-eventful and cooperative relationships with the tax bureau ever after.

Also, late in 1980, the bilateral air agreement between the United States and China was signed, which provided the authority for both the CAAC and Pan Am to initiate twice-weekly flights. A further clause allowed them to grow to three per week during the next two years, and to six per week thereafter.

On January 7th, 1981, the CAAC wheeled their newest 747 airplane, N1304E, up to the jetway to take on a load of passengers bound for the United States. It was the inaugural flight for the CAAC, initiating a service that had never before existed in the history of the two countries—direct flights by Chinese-owned airplanes piloted by Chinese crews. Far more than symbolic, the new service began the actual bridge that had been only words in diplomatic circles since early in 1979.

A gala reception was held at the airport, hosted by Mr. Shen Tu, director general of the airline, with invited guests Ambassador and Mrs. Woodcock beaming their pleasure. A huge red and white banner, proclaiming the event, was unfurled in front of the plane, and bouquets of flowers were presented to the captain and his crew. At 11:26 a.m. local time, N1304E began its roll, taxied quickly out, and climbed into history.

Three weeks later, on January 27, 1981, Pan Am began service. The China Clipper, after an absence of forty years, but this time a 747, appeared once again in the skies over China.

CHAPTER 13

WE BRACED FOR a bitter winter in 1981, our second, but were pleasantly surprised. With milder weather, we escaped the Beijing Lung, perhaps having become acclimatized, and at the airport the CAAC operations began to show a smoother cadence. Winters in Beijing were never easy, however, and with the airplanes parked on the flight line during the night, the freezing problem overtook the Chinese as soon as the weather turned cold.

Freezing of the 747 fresh water system could easily have been avoided if the Chinese had transplanted their 707 experience to the 747 fleet. It was altogether incongruous in view of the fact that for nearly eight years they had been operating 707s with a similar system. The only logic that stimulated them appeared to be the logic of cost, particularly when it involved the outlay of hard cash.

Traditionally, at least under the Communist regime, the Chinese work as isolated units, with only vertical communication, oblivious to others working in close proximity, in fact suspicious and secretive. Thus, the new 747 maintenance team formed in February 1980, when the first airplane arrived, was obliged to learn with little benefit from their 707 compatriots. Indeed, they operated almost as separate airlines.

When a 747 returned to home base at Beijing, the crew routinely signed it over to the maintenance team, who completed a post-flight inspection, replenished the engine oil and drained the excess water, then assigned the plan to the security section.

Security was handled by the army, young men, many without even middle-school education, whose sole concern was to keep anyone from coming near the airplane. They insisted that all external openings be closed and secured, including the panels covering the water-drain valves. The maintenance personnel, on the other hand, anxious to go home after the late night flights, would close the drain valves prematurely, leaving sufficient water in the lines to form an ice plug. The next morning the airplane could not be serviced with fresh water until the ice was melted, which resulted in flight delays and sometimes cracked parts. It took almost two years to get the procedure changed. Finally, for the winter of 1982, security was directed to leave the access doors open, wiring them to avoid damage in the wind, and likewise to leave the drain valves open during the night.

We laughed at superstition, and on Friday the 13th of March left for Bangkok, for our second trip out of China. We found that the Chinese also have many superstitions, perhaps more than we in the West. Unaccountably for an atheistic society, they consider 13 unlucky, leaving it out of the floor-numbering system in most multi-storied buildings.

Our trip to Bangkok was uneventful—almost. We were invited to the first-class cabin even though our tickets were economy class. The airplane was configured with ten first-class seats, and there were only three passengers in the entire section when we departed from Beijing. The plane stopped at Guangzhou on the way, and a group of seven Chinese military men came on board, filling the first-class section. They all wore *mao* caps and the standard, baggy, ill-fitting, green cotton uniforms typical for Chinese military personnel—with no indication of rank. Everyone was equal, even in the military—at least to the casual observer.

To our surprise, as we debarked, a platoon of Thai Air Force officers, resplendent in full-dress uniforms, were lined up in formal salute. Nearby was a reviewing stand with a full military honor guard, complete with brass band. Later we were told that the "military men" who had boarded at Guangzhou included the Chief of Staff of the Chinese Air Force.

In the fourth modernization, that of defense, attention is being paid to returning rank insignia to the uniforms of the military units. There have been reports of disaster in battles along the China-Vietnam border as a result of poor identification of command. The PLA has resisted such changes; however, Deng appears to be firmly pushing the reforms.

On Easter Sunday, the newly formed Beijing Foreign Community Christian Church congregation made a pilgrimage to the Great Wall for Easter sunrise services. A do-it-yourself congregation, operating without a minister except on random occasions, was the result of strong personal efforts by Pamela Indahl, wife of the U.S. Embassy Security Chief, eventually including Christians from more than twenty countries. It was believed to be the first Easter sunrise service ever held at the Great Wall by foreign Christians.

The temperature was 35 degrees F, with a brisk breeze on a clear morning, with the sun suddenly breaking over the hills in the vicinity of the east parapet of the Wall.

Also in April, we had the opportunity to visit the Peking Man site. The diggings are in and around an extensive limestone deposit. Not well versed on the discovery, I retreated to my history books to learn the details. At dusk on December 2, 1929, a well-preserved skull of a primitive man was excavated on Dragon Bone Hill near the town of Zhoukoudian, a suburb of Beijing. Scientific identification showed that it belonged to a new type of apeman who lived about 500,000 years ago.

In 1953 a museum was established at the site. In 1961 the Chinese government designated the place as one of China's major government-protected cultural sites. In 1972 a new exhibition hall was erected.

Fossil remains of Peking Man unearthed at Zhoukoudian include 6 complete skulls, 9 skull fragments, 6 pieces of facial bones, 15 mandibles, 152 teeth, and 7 fragmented limb bones, belonging to upward of 40 persons. Dimensions of the cave home of Peking Man were estimated to be 140 meters east-west and 40 meters north-south. When found, the cave was filled with layers of deposits more than 40 meters thick. Weathering and erosion had erased all but traces of the roof that once covered a large part of the cave.

Descending into the excavation, we had the feeling of retrograding 500,000 years as we studied the 13 layers of overburden, each with a different visual pattern. We encountered Chinese children in droves. The visit was a standard field trip for the schools. They eyed us curiously, but, like all Chinese children, were well behaved. I supposed they were looking for the horns on the "foreign devils."

By good fortune, the Peking Man site had been embraced by the Mao regime as a useful historical treasure. As such, it escaped the ravages of the marauding Red Guards. Many of China's ancient creations did not fare so well. The walls around nearly all the cities succumbed to the intensity of the rejection of all things old, as did many other artifacts as well. The recognition and acceptance of ancient Chinese history and culture became one of the fresh manifestations of the modernization program.

Returning to the city, we stopped at Luguo (Marco Polo) Bridge. The bridge, spanning the Yongding River, is famous as the place where the Chinese began the war of resistance to the invading Japanese, in what is known historically as the Luguo Bridge Incident of July 7, 1937.

The bridge is also famous for its longevity. Built of stone in the 12th century, it was not exactly new when Marco Polo visited. A long span, 260 meters across the meandering river, it has 11 arches. Its stone balustrades include 140 sculptured balusters on either side, with a lion carved at the top of each, no two of which are the same.

The competition between the Boeing 737 and the McDonnell Douglas DC 9 became more intense. The Chinese again postponed a decision, creating a large evaluation team and requesting that Boeing bring an airplane to China to demonstrate its performance on the Chengdu-Lhasa route and on a number of short and unimproved airfields.

During the summer of 1981, negotiations for a 737 airplane demonstration in China were going forward, and a tentative date of mid-September was established. In the interim, Beth and I made ready for our first home leave to the United States. The prospect of returning home again after seventeen months in the alien environment of China was an overwhelming anticipation. We felt as if we were going back to the "world."

Our departure date of June 25th was based not only on the Boeing 18-month rule but also on the IRS requirement for remaining in a "hardship" area for 510 consecutive days in an 18-calendar-month period, in order to qualify for preferential tax treatment.

We returned to China on the 17th of August, refreshed and renewed. Back at the job, I was advised of an incident that had occurred in Guangzhou on June 30, a few days after I had departed. A scheduled 707 flight was preparing to land in low clouds and fog. As the plane broke into the clear, the pilot discovered that the plane was to the right of the runway. Ailerons were used to correct this, but the left wing was still down when they landed. Both nacelles on the left side struck the runway with heavy force, sustaining major damage. The left wing was sprung upward, over a half an inch. Shear distress was visible in the front spar web for the total distance between the number one and number two engine positions.

Returning in August, I was pleased and a little surprised at the excellent workmanship that the Chinese had performed. They had replaced an entire section of the spar web, making two structural splices, and the subsequent optical check confirmed normal wing alignment. The event was positive proof that the Chinese, in spite of difficulties, had learned to handle complex repairs.

CHAPTER **14**

EVERYONE EAGERLY ANTICIPATED the demonstration of the Boeing 737 airplane in China, scheduled for September 16 to 21, 1981, by far the biggest event of the year for the CAAC. Boeing leased an airplane already in revenue service in Micronesia to avoid flying one all the way across the Pacific. The chosen bird was Chief Detudamo, one of Air Nauru's "Little Giants," a six-year-old thoroughbred 737-200C, with 14,000 flight hours.

The "C" model incorporated the feature of convertibility. By a rapid conversion of the interior it could be used as all passenger, partial cargo, or all cargo. The airplane was also equipped with a rough field kit, proved useful by many airlines operating from gravel, grass, sand, dirt, and coral runways on six continents. The Chinese had also become interested in the rough-field landing features of the 737 airplane because of the diversity of runway features in the various locations of their vast country.

During the tour, the airplane visited seven cities in six days and made twenty-five flights from short, hot, high, and rough airfields without a pause. The CAAC technical team of fifteen men chosen from many disciplines, who accompanied the airplane throughout its tour, were surprised and pleased at its performance.

Leaving Hong Kong on Wednesday, September 16, the plane came directly out of commercial service and flew to Beijing.

With the CAAC airline covering six regions, the demonstration was scheduled to visit four of them—all but the northeast and northwest regions of Shenyang and Lanzhou.

For the Beijing demonstration, the airplane flew 341 passengers and technical personnel during four flights on Thursday. Later in the day, a ground cargo conversion demonstration was carried out, and hundreds of additional people were conducted through the airplane.

On Friday morning I joined the team as a working member, and we flew to Wuhan, a major industrial complex in central China. A city of 4 million people, with a tiny airfield only 4,500 feet in length, Wuhan was interested in acquiring medium-range airplanes. Because of its outstanding short-field take-off and landing capability, the 737 showed excellent performance out of Wuhan, even on a hot day, a result which amazed the Chinese evaluation team.

The next stop was Chengdu, gateway to Lhasa Tibet, and the centerpiece of the demonstration tour. The Chinese viewed flying to Lhasa as a nearly impossible feat for a twin jet. The route from Chengdu presents an unbroken chain of jagged peaks with a mean altitude of some 14,000 feet, where, a few hundred miles to the south, the Himalayas stand as silent sentinels, warning the flier not to stray too far from the air corridor.

In 1981 the CAAC was still flying the IL-18 four-engine Russian-built turboprop, because four engines were "more safe." The Chinese were at first petrified by the audacity of the plan to fly a twin jet into those forbidding mountains, and ultimately overwhelmed at the ease with which the Little Giant accomplished it.

Leaving Chengdu at 0700 hours on Saturday, September 19, to beat the ground fog and to be able to clear the Chengdu ramp for the early afternoon arrival of the King of Sweden, Chief Detudamo made the 808-mile trip to Lhasa in 1 hour and 49 minutes. Flying at 32,000 feet, the plane shaved a full hour from the commercial schedule. With no fuel at Lhasa, the airplane was required to carry round-trip fuel. In addition to the large fuel load, an operational analysis proved that the 737 had the capability to fly a full load of 115 passengers on the Chengdu-Lhasa-Chengdu route.

Lhasa, the "Shangri-la" of the movie "Lost Horizon," draws the traveler to its heart like a magnet. Thus, the Chinese had great expectations for future tourist traffic to the ancient city. However, of even greater significance, the airplane performance to Lhasa was used as a gauge for its evaluation for suitability throughout China. Indeed, the Chinese were unrealistically preoccupied with the importance of the Lhasa route in selecting an airplane for their vast, diverse, domestic system. Upon the return from Chengdu, the 737 was host to hundreds of viewers, as it opened its doors to interior inspection on the ramp.

After Lhasa, the remainder of the tour was anticlimactic; Chengdu to Shanghai, Shanghai to Guangzhou, Guangzhou to Zhanjiang and return, finally leaving the PRC for Hong Kong on Monday, September 21. I left the team at Guangzhou and returned to my station in Beijing.

The CAAC evaluation team had been working for several months, but in China there are many factors—and factions—to consider. Decisions do not come easily—nor quickly. A primary concern of the Chengdu Region of the CAAC, who would have responsibility for any airplane flying into Lhasa, and also of the CAAC headquarters personnel, was the "vulnerability" of a two-engine airplane to loss of power in one of the engines. Boeing had offered to cut out one engine halfway between Lhasa and Chengdu and show how the plane was able to maintain its altitude after drifting down to 18,000 feet, as ample margin over the Lhasa/Chengdu corridor. The Chinese would not hear of it. However, they agreed to the shut-down on the next leg, over the relatively flat country between Chengdu and Shanghai. The plane performed exactly as predicted.

Nevertheless, the Chinese decided that they would simply forbid the use of a two-engine airplane over the Tibetan mountains, and began preparations for the day when they would initiate 707 service to replace the aging IL-18 turboprops, an event which became a reality in December, 1983.

While the CAAC evaluation team retreated to their offices to argue the merits of the various potential aircraft available to them, life at the operating level went on as usual.

There was no doubt that the Chinese were learning—and improving. However the age-old hangups continued to haunt them. Preventive maintenance had not yet been given the priority it deserved. The Chinese preferred to solve problems. Further, they were averse to doing anything extra unless there was a direct threat to safety—or evidence that it would cost them more by not doing the work.

One of the standard precautions and good maintenance practices to assure that the seals in the landing gear oleo cylinders remain in good condition for a long time was to wipe the exposed chromium plated surfaces of the inner cylinders with an approved oil between every flight—or, better still, both before and after. Followed faithfully, this practice assured that grit and dust getting into the sliding seal would be minimized or eliminated.

When the Chinese finally agreed to this practice, they substituted gasoline in place of oil to wipe the struts. I cautioned them that gasoline would dry out the seals, virtually guaranteeing that they would leak prematurely. Further, gasoline is a fire hazard, its use forbidden by most operators. However, the mechanics found it easier to cut grease and dirt with gasoline and, contrary to their leaders' admonitions, continued the practice. It was only after leaks developed that the mechanics changed to oil. Even then they tried to substitute a Chinese oil, which, judged by sight, smell, and touch, was equivalent. However, when Boeing conducted a laboratory analysis, it was found that the oil caused the seals to shrink rather than to swell. As a result, the Chinese substitute oil was not used.

One day in October, the chromium plating began to peel from the inner cylinder of the left-wing landing gear of one of the 747 airplanes. Although the cause was most probably defective plating at the factory, there was a distinct possibility that improper cleaning of the struts had aggravated the condition. Repair necessitated removal of the entire landing gear from the airplane, which was followed by disassembly to separate the inner cylinder and by sending it back to the factory for replating. The extensive and costly procedure served notice to the Chinese of the necessity of preventive maintenance.

Shortly after that incident, the mechanics began wiping the oleos with an approved oil before every flight. The specter of cash outlays in the future loomed large in the minds of their leaders. However, that diligence was not shared by the line people, and the procedure lasted about a month. The mechanics quickly fell back into their old habits. After fighting their procedure for over a year, I decided to ignore it. The continual reminder on every flight became too much of a burden.

Another shortsighted policy—that of locating all spare parts in Beijing for both the 707 and 747 fleets—also proved to be costly and frustrating. Because of the old guards' penchant for central control, dissemination of parts to other bases simply was never considered on its merits, in spite of my constant urging. I had also strongly recommended the carrying of selected parts as on-board flight spares kits. My suggestions were always taken kindly but condescendingly. The Chinese would thank me and then remark, "Yes, you are right, Mr. Bauer, it is a good idea, but in China we. . . ." It took several years for the Chinese to stop giving this "spring loaded" response, but, to their credit, they gradually began to accept new ideas, adopt them, and move forward. By 1984 that phrase had disappeared from their vocabulary.

Eventually, as a result of a number of serious flight delays, which could have been prevented by the use of on-board kits, they took my advice, and in the fall of 1981 began carrying spares kits on all the 707 and 747 airplanes. Further, they stationed selected critical spare parts at Shanghai and Guangzhou, way points for many of the flights. However, lack of lateral communication proved to be their undoing in many instances. No one knew where the spare parts were except the central control people in Beijing.

On one occasion in late 1981, Flight 102, a money-maker originating in Hong Kong and bound for Beijing, usually fully booked, was canceled because of a component failure. As a result of the new policy, there was a spare in Guangzhou, only twenty minutes away by air. However, Hong Kong did not know about the spare, nor did the flight crew, and, by the time Beijing had reacted, the flight had been canceled. It took four hours to get the spare part to Hong Kong. It was transported by a special flight. Meanwhile, the planeload of passengers was forced to spend an extra night in Hong Kong.

When the winter of 1982 arrived, the Chinese had finally solved the freezing problem in the fresh-water supply system by leaving the drain valves open during the night. However, the unprotected ramp was a very inhospitable place to work during the winter. With temperatures below freezing from mid-November until mid-March, occasionally dipping to -20 C, and with intermittent 60-knot winds whipping down from Siberia, the mechanics faced a difficult, onerous task.

Completion of the 747 hangar was delayed another year, victim of a capital shortage. The completion date was set for

May 1983, a date which slipped to November 1983, and again to January 1984. When the hangar was finally put into service in the summer of 1984, the total delays from the original plan amounted to more than three years.

The hangar was representative of many projects throughout China that were stretched out. Two years into the modernization program, the faster moving economy resulted in demand for consumer goods outstripping the supply. Thus, 1981 was a year of retrenchment, government policies focusing on a balanced budget and curbing inflation. The budget deficit was deliberately held down from 1980, and budget austerity contributed to a slowing in national income growth. Falling investment and decreased demand led to a further unplanned drop in heavy industrial production; however, light industry continued to register large gains.

In 1979 Deng, emphasizing more consumer goods for the masses, had called for a brake on 120 large-scale projects that had been drawn up in 1978 under the leadership of Hua Guofeng. One of the major projects to suffer was the $5 billion Baoshan Steel Works being built by the Nippon Steel Company near Shanghai. Even the PLA funds were cut, touching the nerve of the hardliners.

Bad news multiplied. Mother Nature was uncooperative, indeed downright nasty in 1981. On the North China plain, the two-year drought tightened its grip, causing many summer crops to be abandoned—plowed under. In the south and east, vast areas were flooded in the basins of the Yellow and Yangtze Rivers. The Chinese reported for the first time in more than a decade that some people had died of starvation, and appealed to the United Nations for food relief.

CHAPTER 15

THE YEAR 1981 proved to be a time of severe testing for China's new leaders, and the Maoists, still strong in the ranks, clamored for a reversal of Deng's accommodative economic policies.

During the year, the Chinese first began to realize the rationalization of their economic structure, the economic management system, and an organizational concept through readjustment and reform. Progress was noted in culture, education, and science, which bode well for advancements in production, technology, management, and economic growth. The standard of living for the nation as a whole was raised.

Heavy industrial growth was intentionally slowed, and the growth rates of agriculture and light industry were accelerated. Per capita income varied widely, with a 1981 figure of $130/year for rural people and $275/year for office and factory workers. The leadership remained uncautiously optimistic, predicting a national average of $1,000/year by the turn of the century.

Industrial output tilted heavily toward consumer goods, with coal, natural gas, and oil dropping, while motor vehicle, bicycles, and sewing machines dramatically increased.

Following the Third Plenum of the Chinese Communist Party's Central Committee, the Party gradually mapped out the "correct road" to socialist modernization, suited to China's conditions.

Ten pointers to modernization were announced:

"Since socialist reformation has basically been completed, our main problem is the discrepancy between people's increasing material and cultural needs and current production. The focal point of the Party's and the government's work must be shifted to socialist modernization, with emphasis on economic construction.

"Economic construction must proceed according to China's needs and resources. Both impatience and excessive patience should be avoided.

"Economic reform must be realistic and compatible with current levels of mechanization and technology.

"Since the exploiting classes have been effectively eliminated, class struggle is no longer a major concern. We must unite all available forces so as to maximize our national effort.

"We must develop a socialist political system with a high degree of democracy. Our Constitution and legal system should be perfected and made inviolable. The turmoil of the 'Cultural Revolution' must not be repeated.

"Proper attention should be paid to science, education, and culture, which can play an important role in socialist modernization.

"Understanding and cohesion among the various nationalities should be enhanced, as befits the socialist society.

"We must continue to strengthen our national defense, maintaining the ties of the armed forces with the government as well as with the people.

"We must carry on the struggles against imperialism, hegemonism, colonialism, and racism, and so maintain world peace.

"Our Party's style of work is of vital importance, We must develop democratic procedures based on the Marxist ideal of collective leadership. Any form of personality cult must be prohibited."

Conflict clearly showed, even though masked in a careful choice of words. The new strongman, diminutive Deng Xiaoping, was straining mightily to maintain the momentum of his modernization program, while being sniped by a powerful left, still firmly entrenched in the PLA and the old guard in the Central Committee. However, the fragile glue of the four modernizations held. The crucial turning point had passed. From that time, Deng's locomotive of economic readjustment and reform remained squarely on the tracks, and China seemed determined never to turn back.

A major contributing milestone was the completion of the trial of the Gang of Four in 1980. The leader, Jiang Qing, Chairman Mao's headstrong widow, was sentenced to death, but sent to prison instead.

The new leniency was pragmatic and purposeful. Mao was still widely revered throughout China, and the execution of his widow would be regarded as a dishonor to his name. The new leadership was anxious to show the world that they had progressed beyond the principle of an eye-for-an-eye, and that their courts of justice were firmly in place and capable of making balanced judgments. Perhaps most important was to defang the leftist desire of obtaining a martyr who would serve as a rallying point. By sparing Jiang Qing, the new government reinforced its image of moderation and self-confidence, preserving unity and stability in the country.

Agricultural reform, the first of the four modernizations, was showing measureable progress. In fact, rural change was sweeping aside one of Mao Zedong's most cherished institutions, the farm communes that the late Communist leader intended to be homes, workplaces, and political centers for the peasants.

The idea that no member of the commune should work harder or earn more than the others—shared poverty—was giving way to the concept that individual enterprise, initiative, and productivity should be rewarded. The first crack had appeared in the "iron rice bowl."

By 1982 communes were beginning to fade out. A sharp rise in agricultural production rendered them outmoded, as individual households again begame the basic farming unit.

James Wallace, chief of the Beijing Bureau of *U.S. News and World Report,* traveled thousands of miles throughout the Chinese countryside during 1982 to see the changes firsthand.[1] He found more and more family units, even individuals, doing tasks that were formerly the responsibility of the entire commune. Land had become available to workers willing to sign production contracts or to join other private enterprise-style systems. Cooperatives and corporations were allowed to process and sell whatever contractors had agreed to produce. According to Wallace, "Above quota output belongs to the tiller or the toiler."[1]

The revolutionary changes on the farms do not mean that Beijing equates private enterprise with capitalism. There is no plan to surrender the Communist Party's power in the countryside. The most common complaint of the Party's hardliners is that the farmers who grow crops to be sold for cash sooner or later will turn into bosses who behave like landlords, and hire others to do their dirty work. They warn that reforms create contradictions and threaten the Communist system. However, the ruling hierarchy is careful not to suggest such deviations. Instead, they point to the "correct socialist principle" of distribution, i.e., "from each according to his ability, to each according to his work."[2]

The hard-line leftists equated being rich to exploiting others: i.e., someone became poor as a consequence. The idea that everyone could be rich began to take root and by 1984 had gained official sanction as a commendable goal.

What happens to the rationalization of ideology and the fu-

---

[1] *U.S. News and World Report,* January 17, 1983.
[2] Article 6, Constitution of the PRC, December 4, 1982.

ture road that China will follow remains to be seen, but the reforms begun in Sichuan were the basis for extending them throughout China, and their architect, Premier Zhao Ziyang, climbed the ladder of power based on that success.

According to Wallace, for the vast majority of peasants in the rice-bowl provinces such as Sichuan life was still mostly a day-to-day grind of transplanting rice seedlings in the chilly, knee-deep water, tilling the fields with heavy hoes, shivering or sweltering in dimly lit homes, and eating simple food.

A peasant's home may be nothing more than a cave in a clay hillside, a mud-brick hut, or a simple prefabricated building. Electric fans to ease the discomfort of blistering summers were rare. In winter's cold, heat other than from a primitive stove, used only to cook meals, was a luxury.

Wallace saw evidence of a brighter future under the new system as he toured Sichuan's Qionglai county, an area where contract farming was pioneered. There, individual enterprise by farmers was paying off in brick houses, some with two-burner stoves and lamps using energy from biogas generators.

He cited a young farmer, Gu Yueming, aged 30, and his 27-year-old wife Li Shiying. They farmed slightly less than an acre of fertile bottomland under a contract, renewed annually, that gave Gu exclusive use of the plot of State-owned land. His contract called for him to turn over a fixed quota of grain to the Phoenix Integrated Company, which absorbed 40 communes in 1979. Any surplus from Gu's labor was his own.

Gu's total yearly earnings from his commune a decade earlier amounted to just $40 in cash and "enough grain to get by on." In 1979, when rural reform began taking hold in Qionglai, his cash income rose to $250.

Through hard work and more extensive use of fertilizer and pesticides, Gu's output in 1982 rose to 5 tons of grain, of which 2 tons of rice and 1.2 tons of wheat were delivered to Phoenix to fulfill his contract. By selling the surplus of 1.8

tons or using it to fatten pigs for the market, and by producing yeast for the local distillery, the family's one-year cash income topped $2,000.

When they were married in 1973, the young couple lived in a cramped mud-brick dwelling. By 1982 the family had a school-age son and a daughter, with a 1,440 square-foot house made of kiln-dried bricks that cost $4,000 for materials and outside labor. They owned two bicycles, two wristwatches, a cassette player, and some new furniture, and they had plans to buy a 14-inch TV set for which they would pay $635.

The Phoenix collective had a unit that did the plowing for everyone. But Gu and his wife did their own seeding, transplanting of rice shoots, and harvesting. He and his three neighbors jointly owned an $80 foot-powered threshing machine that saved labor and reduced waste.

Another experiemnt began in 1979, when 26 inefficient, money-losing communes were turned over to the Yangtze River Agriculture, Industry, and Commerce Corporation near the World War II capital of Chungking (now Chongqing). In just under four years, it had become a Chinese-style conglomerate, with wholly owned subsidiaries, shareholders, contract workers, and joint ventures.

With progress in agriculture proceeding extremely well in 1982, additional attention was directed to the second and third modernizations, industry and science, still in the embryonic stage. Taking things in order, the Chinese intially concentrated on industrial reforms. As a first step in 1980, four special economic zones were established—Shenzhen, Zhuhai and Shantou (Swatow) in Guangdong Province, and Xiamen (Amoy) in Fujian Province.

Shenzhen, Zhuhai, Shantou, and Xiamen were chosen as special economic zones in part because people in these places have a great many overseas connections and a tradition of interaction with the outside world. As zones they were opened wider to the outside than other parts of China and allowed to offer preferential terms to foreign investors so as to concentrate capital and introduce world-advanced technical and managerial skills.

To some extent the zones were intended to act as filters between China's socialist system and the capitalist world, allowing market mechanisms and the law of value to operate under the guidance of the socialist planned economy, taking in what was considered to be positive aspects and sifting out negative aspects of Western culture. The zones were also intended to help promote China's restructuring of economic and managerial systems by acting as laboratories for pilot projects and then passing on successful experiences to the whole country.

The Chinese view the special economic zones as quite different from the "processing zones" and "free zones" set up in some developing capitalist countries, despite the fact that they have some common aspects, such as favorable terms given to foreign investors, a relatively free interflow of foreign funds and personnel, emphasis on the processing and basic manufacturing industries, and export promotion.

Further, the zones were intended to go far beyond merely a method of providing employment, gaining foreign exchange, and promoting local prosperity. Indeed, a major purpose is to introduce technology-intensive, knowledge-intensive, and capital-intensive enterprises for China's long-range benefit. Although the industrial structure is dominated by production for export, a supplementary factor is the manufacture of advanced products for the domestic market.

While "processing zones" in other countries engage only in processing and manufacturing for export, China's zones, such as Shenzhen and Xiamen, are aimed at all-round growth in industry, agriculture, tourism, science, technology, and culture. The zones were expected to become doors for economic and technical cooperation and cultural exchanges between China and other countries, and bridges between those places and the interior regions of China.

By 1984 the State Council, in reviewing the progress in the special economic zones, took a second important step in authorizing fourteen coastal cities to open economic zones. These were to be less than full-fledged special economic zones, but would practice certain policies in common, such as tax incentives for foreign investors.

The overall guideline for these developments was stated by Party Secretary General Hu Yaobang: "Handle special affairs in a special way, and new matters in a new way. The methods may be novel, but our orientation remains the same."[3]

The efforts in industrial modernization initiated in the coastal area of China were only a dent in the surface, however, steps were being considered to broaden them.

There was much talk about a new science, which the Chinese called "talentology." An association was created to further this science, which is unheard of in other countries. The purpose was to do something about the waste of men and women of ability and special training that has been going on in China for over thirty years.

Foreign-educated Chinese scientists, sociologists, and economists had been relegated to language teaching or translating. All young men and women were told to study whatever the State wanted them to study, and do whatever work they were assigned, regardless of individual talent or interest.

Ever since the formation of the People's Republic in 1949, individualism had been criticized and conformity encouraged. The "cog-in-the-wheel mentality" was considered to be the highest possible achievement, since it submerged the individual in the collective.

[3]*China Reconstructs,* September 1984.

When wall posters were permitted on Democracy Wall in 1978 and 1979, one poster writer asked why, in their own country, Chinese could not develop to their full potential and yet, after they went abroad, they sometimes became Nobel Prize winners.

I found that foreigners were definitely not trusted, even foreigners dedicated to contribute to China's development or individuals under contract, as I was, to provide technical help in very specialized fields. Before normalization, and even after, people could be imprisoned for giving information to foreigners. The classification of "State secrets" could be applied to any document or paper that the authorities chose to so classify, particularly after it became convenient or expedient to do so. Indeed, routine economic data and production figures might be classified as "State secrets" at some bureaucrat's whim.

Further, Chinese who were not Party members were considered to be less trustworthy than those who were. They could be accorded outward respect, or public honor, but they had no power and became ineffectual because they were not trusted. In some cases, even Party members were not trusted. Perhaps they had gone to missionary schools or studied overseas, and then returned to China. Or they might have had relatives in Hong Kong or Taiwan. Even veteran Party members were not trusted. If they had been arrested by the Nationalist forces, they could remain under suspicion long after. Others who worked underground for the Communists might not be trusted because they lived in large cities and were subjected to bourgeois temptations for many years. They might have secretly succumbed.

The most trustworthy Party members were those who started with the Revolution, particularly those on the Long March. The majority came from peasant stock and had little or no formal education. Trained as guerrilla fighters in the 1930s and 1940s, they were the most disciplined and became the leaders of the Party, still holding crucial posts in the eighties, even though many were of advanced age, some even senile.

Normalization was bound to nourish forces which contributed to the dichotomy of a closely regulated and controlled society with the behavior of its individual members, as interactions with the Western countries proliferated on all fronts.

The most celebrated case was the defection of Hu Na, China's premier woman tennis player, in July 1982. With that incident culminating in the granting of asylum by the United States, the Chinese were faced with the reality of potential defections in large numbers. One of the immediate reactions was to strengthen security measures as well as to select only those individuals with "very high ideological standards" for activities in foreign countries. Further, the intensity of the political training both before and after overseas missions was amplified.

I was witness to the process about one year later. In the summer of 1983, an associate with whom I worked, and who was fluent in English, was selected for an assignment in England. He was a young man in his early thirties, an enterprising member of the Communist Party, and he was sent to work on a technical program in England for about two months. Upon the day of his return, he came to my office, very happy to be back home.

"How did you like England?" I inquired after the usual welcoming greetings.

"Oh, England was very enjoyable. There are a lot of new things there."

A week later, when asked about England by an associate in the CAAC, my friend stated that he found it to be a nice place to visit, but definitely would not want to live there.

Still later, I attended a luncheon banquet hosted by officials of the CAAC, which my friend also attended. When asked how he liked his trip to England, he was emphatic in his reply: "I didn't really like it at all. I went simply because it was my assignment." Then he added with a laugh, "My boss sent me."

Clearly, the legacy of rigid control for centuries has left a deep cultural imprint upon the Chinese people. The process of change, although given a dynamic start by the modernization program was destined to be slow.

With progress in the special economic zones showing the way, early in 1983 the new leaders made the firm decision that the philosophy of incentive production, also proved on the farms, should be applied to the industrial and commercial sectors throughout China. New directives were issued to substitute taxation of enterprises rather than to collect all their profits.

In 1983 even the intellectuals were liberated, at least in principle, when Hu Yaobang, Secretary General of the Communist Party, stated that from then on the first requirement for selecting cadres would be whether they possessed knowledge of modern science and culture.

At the CAAC I began to notice the new policies in action on a daily basis, or at least trying to be born. It was extremely difficult. The harvest of thirty years of mistrust of individuals and of indifference to progress had produced a quagmire of inefficiency, reluctance to change, inability to communicate, fear of expression, absence of initiative, disinterest in established goals, and individual hoarding of goods and information. It was the same throughout China. In spite of these hardships and hazards, I felt I could see green shoots. There were bright areas, like small patches of winter wheat on the gray landscape of November.

I became convinced that for a people who could aim an arrow straight to the horizon of their goals, ignoring the pits and chasms along the way, success was probable. The Chinese had demonstrated throughout their history that they possessed a tenacity and a stoic acceptance of hardship which would make it happen, no matter how long it took.

CHAPTER 16

Everything in China has a level, a code, a number, a degree, or some other simplified categorizing index. Work is organized into cells or units. Charters are established for the limits and bounds of authority of each unit. Output is designated. Remuneration is controlled in carefully ladled levels. Punishments are precisely catalogued. Careers are meticulously arranged, marriages forbidden or condoned. Retirement is rigidly specified. Above all, population control is layered with rewards and penalties.

A technique that the Chinese have found useful for conditioning and molding the opinions of the people is the copious use of slogans, a practice that might be called "sloganology," nearly a science in itself.

Having bowed to the wills of emperors for centuries, and more recently to the preachings of Mao Zedong, with the red book prescribing a formula for every occasion, the average Chinese had a mind that was "bent out of shape." It could hardly have been otherwise.

While the rest of the developing world was driving for economic betterment, seeking technology, watching with anticipation the scientific achievements in the Western nations following World War II, China was wallowing in the strains and stresses of consolidating its new revolution. The Great Leap Forward, Mao's answer to the Western challenge, had failed miserably. Then, adding terrible havoc to an already injured, tortured, and backward nation, he unleashed the Cultural Revolution.

During the ten-year period from 1966 to 1976, the few intellectuals who existed were ranked at the lowest level imaginable: below landlords, rich peasants, counter revolutionaries, the bad elements, the rightists, the renegades, the special agents, and the capitalist-roaders—in fact, purged from the mainstream of society. The net result was a "deficiency in intellectual infrastructure," which I named the "DII Factor."

By the beginning of 1982, much progress had been made in overcoming the decades-old bias against intellectuals, but that core of the new modernization program was only slowly being created out of the crucible of debate and acrimony within the Party. A factory worker could, by exceeding his output quota, still make a higher income than an engineer or a member of the university faculty. It was not until 1983 that the first positive measures were taken in the highest ranks of the Party to welcome the intellectuals back into the fold.

Thus, it was inevitable that 1982 was the year of slogans. The ten pointers to modernization became watchwords, replacing the Mao books as a source of guidance. Civic virtues, for example, became a national issue, and March 1982 was declared the first National Civic Virtues Month. *China Daily* reported good results from various parts of the country.

Of the "Three D's"—dirtiness in the environment, disorder in public places, and discourtesy among people in professional services—environmental sanitation improved the most.

According to *China Daily:* "Thousands of tons of refuse, much of which has been accumulating for more than a decade, have been removed from cities and towns. Millions of saplings have been planted in towns and on the outskirts. Beijing, at least, has reported that there is much less spitting in the streets.

"There are notably fewer traffic accidents in the metropolises, with thousands of workers and cadres standing guard in the thoroughfares during rush hours. A better attitude in waiting on customers and commuters has been noticeable among the majority of shop assistants and public conveyance conductors, although quite a few still put on a blank or even a forbidding look."[1]

I can attest to the better attitude. The clerks in the Friendship Store actually began to notice customers, where before they turned their backs so as not to have to deal with them. After all, it took too much time from their gossip with friends or their daydreaming and *xuixi*. If something was not available, they would literally shout a favorite word, *"meiyou"* (don't have), with unbridled glee.

However, it was not the slogans that made the difference; it was the new incentive beyond the standard, small salary. For the first time in their memory, clerks were actually being rewarded for sales and service, not merely being paid to stand for eight hours behind the counters.

Many campaigns were carried out to improve the attitude of shop assistants, but, whenever a campaign was over, they drifted back to their old ways. Recently, in addition to providing monetary incentives, new rules are being enforced to handle the most flagrant abuses. One of the rules states that anyone who strikes a customer will be fired. There are reports of three persons being sacked for this violation in Beijing during the first half of 1984.[2]

The workers and cadres standing guard in the thoroughfares during rush hours were noticeable, primarily because of the special red armbands that the designated brigades were required to wear. However, in the crush of downtown streets like Wangfujing and Xidan in Beijing, the result was like trying to ward off a swarm of bees with a fishnet. And as

---

[1] *China Daily,* April 1, 1982.
[2] *Ibid.,* August 24, 1984.

suddenly as March ended, everyone fell back into the old habits.

Civic virtues went far beyond cleanliness and orderliness in the streets. It included a reawakening or "spring cleaning" of the mind. Brought forward for the consideration of every person were the "Five Graces"—civility, courtesy, tidiness, orderliness, and integrity. Further, there were the "Four Beauties"—cultivate a noble heart, polite language, good manners, and a beautiful environment.

Anything so successful for a month in China deserved to be institutionalized, so a year later, in March 1983, the National Committee for Promoting Civic Virtues was established with a vice-premier as chairman. The committee was composed of leading officials from more than thirty Party and government departments. The committee quickly added another big three, "The Three Loves"—love the motherland, socialism, and the Party.

"Stress must be laid on achieving real results in these activities," Mr. Wan Li, the new chairman of the committee, said, "which must help cultivate devotion to serving the people, bring about closer relations between cadres and the masses, and foster a socialist relationship of unity and mutual help among the people."[3]

There was more. Above all, everyone was given the "Five Basic Guarantees of Life"—food, clothing, medical care, housing, and burial expenses."

The institutionalization of Civic Virtues Month demanded that new slogans be continually invented. Thus, in March 1985 the "Three Don'ts" were announced: don't spit, litter, or write on walls. Recent visitors to China are still shocked by the spitting in the streets, particularly in winter, when Beijing Lung is so prevalent. However, the improvement is dramatic. Dur-

[3] *Ibid.,* April 1983.

ing my first winter in 1980, spitting was so bad that I even hesitated to ride my bicycle in the swarm of commuters. The improvement was achieved by more than slogans. Fines were levied and enforced against offenders, and "no spit" zones have been established in the same way as "no noise zones" and "reduced speed" zones.

Reading the proclamations, I was again reminded of the lack of lateral communication inherent in the Party system, and reflected how serious a barrier this was to the avowed goals of the new committee, perhaps reducing it in practice to hollow words. However, considering the formative posture of many young Chinese minds, sloganeering served a good purpose.

A rosy picture for China's future is not universally shared. Many foreign teachers and news correspondents, having entered China by the score at the beginning of the normalization in 1979, had sufficient experiences to start talking and writing about them in Western newspapers and magazines. Much of the writing did not make for comfortable reading by the Chinese leaders. The first scorcher was printed in *Harper's* in April 1982.[4]

In an article entitled "China Stinks," James Kenneson, who spent a year as a teacher in the city of Zhengzhou, capital of Henan Province, told a grim story. Correctly, Kenneson noted that Zhengzhou "is twelve train-hours and several mental decades from both Shanghai and Peking (Beijing), where most foreigners spend their time."

No doubt the conditions of Zhengzhou were representative of most places before normalization, and remained the same in a majority of them thereafter. However, normalization was never intended to be a magic wand. It was merely a turning point. The goals were grand and far off. Nevertheless, they

---

[4] "China Stinks," by James Kenneson, *Harper's,* April 1982.

were a beginning, no more of a start than required for the longest journey. Deng had the courage to take the first step.

Kenneson reported: "A typical group of apartment buildings consists of eight or ten four-story brick rectangles arranged in two rows. Each building has four doorless entryways along the front, each entryway leading to a set of concrete stairs. At each landing there are two apartments. All decoration is considered decadent, and therefore is not attempted. The dirt courtyard in front of the buildings is a play-and-gossip area where an occasional street vender hawks his wares. The rear area is divided among the tenants and used for vegetable plots and makeshift chicken coops."

The apartment buildings that Kenneson described were typical of those mushrooming in the relatively modern cities of Beijing, Shanghai, and Guangzhou to avoid lateral expansion and loss of precious agricultural land. Perhaps as much as any activity in China, the drab functional buildings epitomized the country's mood. The new policies began slowly to change that mood, which had been one of resigned despair. The people have begun to exhibit a new industriousness, albeit on a scattered and small scale—not merely responding to orders and directives.

Grass was back in vogue. The bare dirt courtyards that Kenneson described were apparent everywhere in Beijing in 1980, but by 1982 were gradually disappearing under grass, trees, and shrubs. Birds have returned. In 1983, the final week of March was proclaimed as "Love the Birds Week" in Beijing. Keeping of birds was deemed as "bourgeois enjoyment" in the ten years of the Cultural Revolution. When we arrived in Beijing in the winter of 1980, there was scarcely a bird to be seen—the result of the massive campaign in the previous several decades to slaughter them. By the spring of 1983, great flocks of crows were in evidence, and many magpies, happiness birds, and sparrows.

Kenneson mentioned a Chinese slogan—"Be Red and Expert." He went on to say, "If some way can be found to implement this slogan by recruiting the brightest and most decent people into the bureaucracy, there's hope for China's future." Precisely! Kenneson could even see the potential in downtrodden Zengzhou. Educated people throughout China, still a timid minority, were talking about the problems that the casting out of the intellectuals had wrought for the country. Thoughtful men inside the ruling group closest to Deng were also dwelling upon this dilemma.

To visualize the magnitude of the task before the Chinese, and to appreciate the great progress already made, one must take a short look back to the early days that Kenneson spoke about. After painting a picture of sadness, rudeness, frustration, and lost hope that he found in China, Kenneson went further.

"Far from exaggerating, I have omitted much pain. I haven't told a hundred stories because their tellers could be traced by their circumstances and punished. I haven't spoken of the dull and lusterless eyes of the people in the streets, such a contrast to the eyes of Hong Kong; nor of the people penned like cattle behind gates until the train arrives, so they must stampede like mad bulls with all their baggage, several hundred yards to catch it before it leaves, all to sit on hard wooden benches while their leaders ride in 'soft bed' compartments with cushions and tea, seats reserved; nor of the scrapes on children's knees unhealed from April till September, festering and sore; nor the darker follies of medicine and education; nor of the bone-gaunt, nearly naked beggar, picking, with an eager finger, at the pink along a watermelon rind he has rescued from the gutter. Far from being hyperbole, this account barely begins to describe the brutality of daily life in China."

In 1982 Fox Butterfield's book, *China, Alive in the Bitter Sea,* also focused on many of the bad aspects of life in China.

My purpose is not to regurgitate all the sadness that was there. It has already been dwelt upon by many writers of the China scene. Rather, I seek to see a plan and purpose in the new direction and to divine if possible whether it is succeeding. True, it is like observing single grains of sand falling through the glass, one at a time; like watching the tide change; or trying to discern the movement of the hour hand on a watch.

I believe the direction, desire, and patience exists in China. It will take a long time. I first suggested 100 years; then in a moment of euphoria I announced a few decades. Now, with more experience, I believe it cannot be measured in years, decades, or centuries, but rather in generations.

Two or three generations of the kind of progress we have witnessed from 1979 to 1985 should bring China into the world economic and technological mainstream. Such progress is of course based on the premise that the population-control measures now in place prove to be successful over the long pull.

In 1979, naysayers on China's prospects were predominant, whereas today some are predicting an overnight transformation. This will not happen.

Steadily, day by day, imperceptible to the casual eye of the impatient visitor, progress was being made in the growth of the national airline, an entity representative of the bow wave of technological integration. Each day I witnessed this algebraic process—three steps ahead and two back, but undeniably progress.

A particular event in February 1982 was especially encouraging. The leading edge of the trailing edge wing flap had been struck by a large bird, inflicting extensive damage. The damage was not repairable in the field, and the assembly required replacement. Of honeycomb core construction, it was adhesively bonded metal, accomplished in an autoclave under heat and vacuum-induced pressure. Edge treatment was provided to allow the part to be attached to the flap structure with multiple fasteners. New assemblies came from the factory undrilled, requiring fitting to the existing structure and drilling to match. The assembly was complex, with two-dimensional curvature, close tolerances, and a critical fit and fair, since it was an aerodynamic surface. I explained the complexity of the task and the care required to do it properly—and waited. From experience, I knew some things were better observed with one's back turned.

A few days later, I inspected the finished job. I was pleased to find an example of precise workmanship, which we in the aircraft manufacturing business had learned to expect and admire. In my mind, this raised the capability potential of the CAAC another increment.

In April the CAAC maintenance team demonstrated how far they had progressed in learning about the 747 airplane and its complex systems. The bus tie breakers in the electrical power network of one of the airplanes had been intermittently tripping for several months. Trouble-shooting by the Boeing technicians had uncovered nothing. Mysteriously, the airplane would fly for one, two, and three weeks, trouble free—and suddenly, during flight, the breakers would all trip, interrupting electrical power on the airplane. The crew would reset the breakers one by one and continue the flight in a normal manner. The tripping was not serious, only a nuisance; nevertheless, we needed to find the cause and make repairs. All the suspected components had already been replaced. Boeing dispatched two electrical engineers to meet the airplane on its overnight stop in New York, to review the wiring system. The engineers gave it a clean bill of health. There appeared to be nowhere else to search.

The Chinese technicians kept at the trouble-shooting. One day they discovered an ever-so-faint indication of arcing in one of the tiny gold-plated pins in a connector. The pin fit loosely in its socket. Boeing conducted a laboratory analysis and found that the connector had its "napkin ring" missing (a small ring that functioned to provide holding pressure). There was no previous record of such a defect occurring in the millions of connectors that had been manufactured. The discovery of that faulty connector was another red feather in the caps of the CAAC maintenance team.

Yet, accountably, in simple things, the Chinese mechanics resisted learning. Certain procedures that they were performing incorrectly they simply would not change. Every morning, when the flights were being prepared for departure, I observed the cargo loaders. I noticed the loading sequence was such that there was no working space in the cargo hold as the last several containers were put in. By changing the sequence slightly, i.e., loading both forward and aft of the doorway, then loading the doorway last, working room would be available to handle the containers until the last one was loaded. I pointed out the preferred sequence to my interpreters. I reviewed it with the loaders. I drew diagrams and discussed them with the crew chiefs. Everyone nodded and smiled. Yes, they said, it was a good idea. The next morning, the crew was back doing the loading the same old way.

All was not work in my support role of the Chinese. The Americans were planning an expedition to Mt. Everest from China in the spring of 1984. I had met the leaders for the climb in Beijing in the summer of 1980 and agreed to act as the liaison for the group in China. It was my introduction to Ultima Thule, the code name of the expedition. The leaders invited me to join them and to climb part way up the mountain.

Thus, in the spring of 1982, after Beth and I returned from a week's rest and relaxation in Tokyo, I revised my physical conditioning program in anticipation of the 1984 event. Always diligent on an exercise regime of swimming, cycling, or jogging, I extended the distance and formalized the activities.

Measuring the distance with an automobile odometer, I fitted in three miles each weekday morning before breakfast, and slightly over five on Sundays. The Sunday jog consisted of a trip around the Forbidden City in central Beijing. On each occasion, I was able to observe many other joggers, hundreds of Chinese doing *tai jiguan,* the national body control exercises, others doing sword maneuvers, old men with their cages of happiness birds, singers practicing near the moat—even people playing musical instruments in the quiet area by the north gate.

One morning, with my mind in a comfortable neutral state and my body moving along at ease, I was startled by the raucous cry of a rooster immediately behind me. Unbelieving, I glanced over my shoulder; coming up fast was a bicycle loaded with racks of live chickens. In the center cage of the crowded mass of wings, legs, and feathers, a little white rooster lifted his head, crowing mightily. That experience became common, and its wonder never ceased—that in Tiananmen Square, before the Heavenly Gate of the Forbidden City, where lingered the ghosts of emperors of centuries gone by, an ordinary barnyard rooster on his way to market raised his voice to announce the new day. For me it was a signal of hope for all of China.

CHAPTER 17

WITH NORMALIZATION, the Chinese quickly cast off their allegiance to Russian and adopted English as their second language. June 1982 marked the first anniversary of the birth of the only completely English-speaking newspaper in China, *China Daily,* published in Beijing. We quickly became dependent upon the little eight-page, standard-size newspaper for our national news, sports news, and local Chinese news.

Although very popular, *China Daily* was China's least-read newspaper, with a circulation of about 700,000 in mid-1983, tiny compared to the 7 million of the official Communist Party organ, *People's Daily.*

The paper broke new ground. It was the first Communist Chinese newspaper to allow commercial advertising. Although it toed the Party line, we were amazed at how tolerant the authorities were in allowing criticism of methods, events, ideas, and even leaders.

The paper was symbolic of the changes in China during the initial years of normalization. Mr. Liu Zunqi, the co-founder and top editor, admitted that any Chinese trying to start an English language daily during Mao Zedong's time would have been denounced and jailed as a capitalist-roader—as he was. But the pragmatic new leaders of China correctly viewed the newspaper as another good way to open doors to the West.

Launching a North American edition of the newspaper in

June 1983, on its second anniversary, Editor Liu said he hoped to build a circulation of 5,000 the first year and 50,000 eventually. When the editor of the *Wall Street Journal* cautioned that it took the *Journal* a half century to reach 50,000, the managing editor, Mr. Feng Xiliang, responded. "We can wait fifty years."[1]

Tian gao huangdi yuan, "The sky is high and the emperor is far away"—I had an opportunity to test that old Chinese saying when I was arranging for airline tickets for Beth and me to travel to Xian for a weekend sightseeing tour. We had always planned eventually to visit Xian, for we were anxious to see the vaults protecting the Qin tomb that were brought to light in 1974.

It was to be our second experience in traveling by domestic flight in China. The Lhasa trip two years before was much more closely programmed, and then we had a high visibility in the CAAC management hierarchy. On the other hand, the Xian trip was a common commercial flight. Thus, it was perhaps more representative of the procedures required for regular domestic air travel.

Planning to leave on Friday, the 18th of June, I started the ticketing process the first week of June, and found no difficulty in purchasing tickets to Xian, one way. Mr. Zhang, my interpreter, said it would be impossible to purchase a return ticket in Beijing in advance. "Round-trip tickets cannot be purchased," he advised, a curious expression of unbelief on his own face. "They are not offered on domestic flights. You must acquire your return tickets in Xian after you arrive."

We had encountered the same problem on our Lhasa trip, but had assumed it was an exception. Seeing my look of disappointment, Mr. Zhang offered a solution. "You could send

---

[1]*Newsweek,* June 13, 1983, p. 47; *China Daily,* June 19, 1985—In June 1985 circulation reached 80,000.

a telex to Xian requesting reserved space," he volunteered.

I felt much better. "Good idea," I agreed. Mr. Zhang called the ticket office. Judging from the tone of his voice, without understanding much of what he said, I knew there was more trouble.

After finally hanging up the phone, Mr. Zhang laughed. "The ticket people say there is no use in sending a telex, because they are never answered."

"How can that be? Xian is part of the CAAC network, is it not?"

"Oh, yes, but there is no penalty for not answering, and the plane will be full anyway. There is no need to spend money on telexes."

"Very practical—for the Chinese—but that means we will be stuck in Xian." I balked.

Mr. Zhang suggested that we check in at the CAAC office in Xian via the interpreter whom we would be hiring when we arrived. "There will be no problem," he predicted with confidence.

"Yes, I've heard about *meiyou wenti* before. That's when I start to worry. I must be back in Beijing on Sunday evening. I cannot take the chance of being stranded in Xian."

I told him "no thanks," refusing to leave Beijing unless I had a pre-arranged reservation to return on Sunday. Feeling somewhat responsible for my welfare, since I was a foreigner supporting the airline, Mr. Zhang made additional inquiries. Finally, after more excited conversation, he told me that the International Offices of the CAAC could make a special request by telex and it would not be ignored—treatment reserved for VIPs. I was pleased with that result, but wondered how the airline could make progress with these tactics.

Freely applying the Chinese saying "The sky is high and the Emperor is far away" to the real world simply means that people declare their own mandate to ignore directives from authorities in direct proportion to the distance away, but inversely proportional to the level of requesting authority.

The Chinese claimed that every stone and brick in Xian had a story behind it. Judging from how the ancient capital has skyrocketed to prominence as a tourist attraction since the vaults surrounding the tomb of Emperor Qin Shihuang were discovered by peasants sinking a well to fight the drought in 1974, it could very well be true.

Xian, a 3,000 year-old city, served intermittently as the capital of China during eleven dynasties, beginning with the Zhou Dynasty in the 11th century before Christ. Under the Tang Dynasty (618-907) Xian was the political, economic, and cultural center of China. It was one of the largest cities in the world during the Middle Ages. In 1982 Xian had a population of 2.5 million and was the capital of Shaanxi Province.

Tourist attractions abound, and a stay of two days is barely adequate to see the major ones. The most impressive are the life-size pottery figures of the legions of warriors and chariots arranged in battle formation to protect their emperor.

Emperor Qin (259–210 B.C.) unified China and completed the Great Wall. During the period of the Warring States over 2,000 years ago, he annexed the six other ducal states to his own, thus founding the Qin Dynasty and giving himself the title of the First Emperor of Qin. Several sections of the Wall had been built, but it was under Qin that many parts were joined.

As was the practice with all emperors, the after-life was considered to be far more important than life on earth. Therefore, a first task was always to plan and begin construction of one's tomb. Emperor Qin conscripted 700,000 laborers and artisans who toiled for thirty-six years in building the tomb. Today the burial mound is unopened, but the vaults of the soldiers are themselves certainly the 8th Wonder of the World.

Xian epitomizes the poles of the continuum of political

thought in China. The hard-liners, and in particular the Cultural Revolutionists, considered all things old as nearly as decadent as Western bourgeoisie capitalism. They invented a slogan which derided the "Four Olds."

Beijing led the way in destroying old things. First to come down was the magnificent wall surrounding the city. The stones were used for building homes and courtyards. Indeed, China under Mao essentially denied its history, setting sail on a new ocean. The two and one-half decades until his death were devoted to tearing down old China and replacing it with the purely functional trappings of the People's Republic. Xian, oldest and perhaps more significant to the history of China than any other location, did not escape.

In 1368, under the first Prince of Qin in the Ming Dynasty, a new city had been built at Xian and a new city wall constructed surrounding it. The walls of the new city were gradually torn down after the place became the site of the Shaanxi Provincial Government in 1949, leaving the north gate as the last relic of the Ming Dynasty architecture in Xian.

The conflict continued. In December 1982 provincial authorities decided to tear down the north gate to make room for a new staff housing development. The demolition was in open defiance of the new State regulations for protection of historical sites and relics, promulgated under the Deng regime, and ignored the protests from local people and cultural circles.

While the controversy heated up, demolition was halted for a few months. Finally, declaring the site to be of negligible historical value, the provincial authorities resumed the methodical destruction of the north gate. When the case was brought to the attention of the Party's central leadership in Beijing, they supported the protectionists and ordered the demolition to cease.

With Beijing 600 miles away, the provincial authorities redoubled their efforts, bringing in over a dozen bulldozers, excavators, and trucks, working around the clock to rush through the demolition of the north gate.[2] *Tian gao huangdi yuan* was still functioning.

Slowly, the seeds of countercurrent to the destruction of historical sites and artifacts began to take hold, and results were seen throughout the country.

In Tibet, where most of the monasteries and shrines had been destroyed, treasures sacked and carted to China, the old relics were gradually returned. In 1983 alone, some 10,000 Tibetan historical artifacts were given back to their rightful owners.[3]

Indeed, the drive to enoble the past and reconstruct its symbols became a national goal. Major projects were planned, anticipating years of intensive effort. Most visible in 1983 was the plan for Xian itself. In October 1983[4] *China Daily* reviewed the new plan for reconstructing and renovating the ancient walls of Xian. It involved repairing the city walls, dredging the moat, completing the ring road outside the walls, and planting trees along both banks of the moat. *China Daily* reported that already over 3,000 workers had begun the repair of the wall from the eastern to the western gates.

Another intriguing development was begun in Xian in 1983 to promote tourism there. Construction began on a small replica city of the Tang Dynasty. It was expected to be the forerunner of many similar representations of the Chinese dynasties throughout the country.

The correctness of the new policy of protecting the old symbols could be witnessed by the flood of tourists pouring into China. The revenue from those visitors was, and will continue to be, one of the greatest sources of foreign currency. In ad-

---

[2] *China Daily*, May 7, 1983.
[3] *Ibid.*, May 16, 1983.
[4] *Ibid.*, October 18, 1983.

dition, tourism sparked a hotel-building flurry, expansion of railroads, and highways—and a boon to the CAAC.

Hotels and guesthouses sprang up in all the major cities, many of which were the result of joint ventures with foreign firms. The first major joint venture hotel in Beijing, the Jianguo, opened its doors in April 1982 and created a sensation. A direct copy of the Holiday Inn in Palo Alto, California, the structure was literally hauled into China piece by piece. Modern and comfortable, with Western cuisine, and in spite of prices double that of the Beijing Hotel, the hotel was an immediate success, generally booked solid weeks in advance during the main tourist season from April to November, and never dropping below 85 percent of capacity, even in the fiercesome Beijing winters. An attractive feature was the first-ever opportunity for tourists and businessmen alike to make reservations directly with the hotel desk locally and by telex from outside China. At all other Chinese hotels, reservations can be made only by a sponsor via the First Service Bureau, and travelers are uncertain where they will be staying, or even if they have accommodations at all, until after they arrive at the airport. Recently, the Chinese leaders have pointed to the Jianguo Hotel as an example to be studied and followed by local Chinese hotels.[5]

There were other serious problems at the Chinese hotels. One of the most basic was simple communication—knowing who was living in the hotel. We had lived in Room 1405 of the Beijing Hotel for nearly two years when, in the spring of 1982, a visitor to the hotel inquired at the information desk for our room number. The reply was *meiyou*.

Following that incident, I approached the information desk one day, presenting a card. "Please tell me if this person is registered," I requested.

[5]*Ibid.*, August 29, 1984.

"Wait a moment, please," replied the desk attendant, taking the card and shuffling into the back room.

Five minutes later, he returned. "He is not in the hotel."

"Please check again. Perhaps he is listed under the first name."

After another long wait I was given the same reply. I took the card, and, waving it in front of the attendant's face, I replied heatedly: "I am this man. I have been in Room 1405 for two years."

I did not check again until nearly a year later. To my surprise, the attendant produced a computer printout. Quickly scanning the list, he readily found my name—in 1405.

According to an official of China Travel and Tourism Administration, 21 hotels and guesthouses with more than 4,000 rooms were built or upgraded during the first three years after normalization. Fifty-eight new hotels were scheduled in the Sixth Five-year Plan period (1981–1985). Forty-one of them, with a total of 10,000 rooms, are being paid for by the State, and 17, with 13,300 rooms, will be backed by foreign funds. Most of the joint venture capital was emanating from Hong Kong; however, some of the investment came from the United States, Australia, Singapore, and Canada.[6]

Although most of the construction was in the large cities, many smaller cities with main tourist attractions are benefitting. Xian started construction on the Golden Flower Hotel in 1983, the first project involving foreign capital in that city. The same capital backing was behind the Golden Flower as the 1,000-room Great Wall Hotel, completed in Beijing in 1984.

Hard cash from tourism increased from $260 million in 1978 to an estimated $1.5 billion in 1984, when over 12 million tourists visited China.[7] Indeed, the tourist boom is spawning

---

[6]*Ibid.*, October 14, 1982; November 14, 1983.
[7]*Ibid.*, October 14, 1982; January 29, 1985.

new tourist cities, located right at or near various sites. In Beijing, a satellite city for tourism was launched in 1983 in the northern suburbs. Named Chanping County Town, it is only 12 miles from the Great Wall and 6 miles from the Ming Tombs, the two most-visited attractions near Beijing. The new town will have hotels with 2,000 rooms, together with restaurants, shopping centers, cultural, recreational, and sports facilities.

Previous to the development of the tourist city, there were no such facilities near the Great Wall or the Ming Tombs, with a 2½-hour train ride or a 2-hour bus trip from downtown Beijing required for the visit. In 1982, 3.3 million tourists viewed the Ming Tombs.[8]

Recently, far to the west in Urumqi, capital of the Xinjiang autonomous region, plans were announced to complete a tourist village by 1987, which will be a showcase for the history, landscape, culture, and architecture of the region. Construction in the village will include hotels and restaurants, much of which will be financed by foreign capital.[9]

Every province and autonomous region in the vast country has its own unique artifacts and history—all potentials for development as major tourist attractions.

China's announced goal of quadrupling its GNP by the turn of the century is to a significant degree dependent on the continued rapid growth of the tourism industry, which touches almost every facet of light industrial production. By the fall of 1984, the bottleneck was no longer lack of hotel space, but the inability of railroads, highways, and, most notably, the airline, to move people about in China. The CAAC realized they were sitting in the catbird seat, but were moving at a pace entirely too slowly to meet the tide.

[8]*Ibid.*, May 28, 1983.
[9]*Ibid.*, January 1, 1985.

CHAPTER **18**

BY THE SUMMER OF 1982, with the CAAC international routes well covered by the combination of the 707 and the 747 airplanes, the airline realized that it was past time to move forward on the upgrading of its domestic fleet.

Central planning, the core of the Communist system, was continuing to prove its inadequacy in meeting the requirements of the airline in a timely and constructive manner. The demonstration flights of the 737 airplane had been made nine months earlier, and the planners had not yet drawn conclusions on replacement of the old aircraft, nor when, where, and how the new machines, once a decision was made, would be utilized.

There was a strong effort inside the airline to replace the 34 inefficient Tridents; however, the reluctance to invest a large sum of money weakened the will of those who were advising bold action. The Tridents still had a book value of $6 million each, although their market value had eroded to one-tenth of that figure. It was clear that they represented virtually unsaleable merchandise, but the financial directors were unwilling to write them off.

I had gained an inkling of the tortuous discussions, the layered reviews, the linear ladder of organizational flow, and all the other elements of a final decision, when earlier in the year I had observed a series of routine operations at the airport.

One morning in April there was an unusual array of flights

preparing to depart. The previous February a second runway had been opened and dedicated with much fanfare. This was a major accomplishment, completely meeting international standards for handling the largest commercial jet airplanes.

On that particular morning, there was a line of six planes waiting to take off—two Tridents, an IL-18, a 707, a 747, and an IL-62. It was a perfect situation for using both runways. However, the orders had already been given to the tower by the central planners—probably sitting in an office downtown—for the operations at the airport. No on-the-scene initiative could be undertaken by the controllers. They had their orders.

To add insult to an already preposterous situation, a 707 was engaged in flight training and making routine touch-and-go landings—of course using the very same runway. Thus, all six airplanes waited, burning expensive jet fuel, while the 707 training airplane made its first touch-and-go.

Watching the proceedings with me was John Hertel, the Pratt/Whitney representative. It was our normal practice to remain at the ramp while the 747 flights took off each morning. "There's plenty of time for another touch-and-go," I joked as we observed the IL-18, third in line, taking off. John gave a weak laugh. Ten minutes passed. Four of the six planes had managed to take off. Suddenly, out of the haze, we saw a plane coming in for a landing. Sure enough, it was the 707 making a second touch-and-go.

The 747, with its four 50,000-pound thrust engines gobbling fuel, was still waiting in line, followed by the four jet IL-62—all this, in a society which prided itself in saving scarce resources, particularly energy.

Twenty minutes elapsed before the last airplane took off. The economic misfortune of the event was that none of it was necessary, and the ultimate tragedy was that nothing would be done to correct the situation for perhaps three to six months.

The deputy director of maintenance stood attentively on the ramp, watching. He took no notes and reported nothing: it was not his job. Also watching were at least twenty maintenance and ground personnel. Of course, none of them would report it, either. To report would put them in double jeopardy. First, they were supposed to be minding their own business, and, second, criticism of the planning unit would be taken unkindly. Our interpreter, watching with us, would never dare to utter a word. Most frustrating of all, the controllers would be reluctant to criticize the planning orders. They could only laugh among themselves, passing the event off as a joke.

My experience told me what would happen: nothing. At least nothing would happen immediately. Several more incidents of a like nature would occur. Eventually, someone in operations would notice all the delays in the take-off records and the increased fuel consumption. An investigation would be launched. A round of meetings would be held, including all departments concerned. Finally, a report would be prepared. The report would move up through successive layers of management. No action would be taken, each layer judging the responsiblity to be that of someone higher. Very likely, the report would reach the desk of the director general himself (similar to a chief executive officer). Since the buck stops there, he would *direct* someone to do something. At that stage, everyone would begin to feel comfortable. There were firm marching orders. A directive would be written that, after approval, would pass down the line via another series of planning meetings.

In the meantime, events would have overtaken the planning bureaucracy, and other serious considerations would have developed. The cycle would begin all over again. I had been unfavorably impressed many times by similar chains of events.

The CAAC had established a goal of qualifying as an FAA approved repair station for aircraft and engines. Mr. Chang Xianyin, chief of the translator unit attached to the airline, had been given the task of translating the voluminous FAA regulations for qualification as a repair station. He devoted a full year to the translation. After completing the job, he spoke to me about it, saying he had drawn up a conceptual organization and a flow diagram.

"Good idea," I observed, shaking his hand in the Chinese fashion. "And what is the status?"

"Well," he said, grinning self-consciously, "it wouldn't flow!" Then he laughed out loud, and I joined him.

"Why was that?"

"Management problems."

In all likelihood, individual unit managers were unwilling to relinquish their authority over a certain function or functions critical to the overall operation of the repair base—a universal problem.

In a self-proclaimed energy-poor nation—at least poorly developed—the Chinese were also blatantly careless in conserving energy, on the one hand, and curiously naive in the way they went about it, on the other.

Elevators in multi-story buildings were restricted in usage, with the slogan of saving electricity. For example, the CAAC headquarters, a 14-story office building, had three elevators. Two were turned permanently off. Thus, huge queues of thirty to fifty people gathered at the busiest time in the morning. It was not important that literally the entire workforce, except those on the lower floors who used the stairs, were habitually late to their desks. The Chinese rationalized this behavior by reminding us: "Electricity is limited while we have plenty of people."

The obvious defect in that philosophy was that it was rooted in antiquity. In the days when most Chinese were uneducated and there were millions of hands, it was true. However, in modern times, those waiting for the elevator represented the most highly educated few—being kept from doing a full day's work.

In another example of misguided energy conservation, drivers were taught to move from low to high gear as soon as the car got rolling—never mind the correct speed—which resulted in burned-out clutches and overworked engines, a latent cost that could far outweigh the small amount of gasoline needed to accelerate properly.

Another common tactic was to rev up the automobile to 100 kilometers per hour, then cut off the ignition and allow the vehicle to coast down to 30. The cycle was repeated over and over, primarily on the long stretches from downtown to the airport. Even buses employed similar procedures, on a different scale. As they approached a bus stop, they would cut the engine and coast in. Whether any fuel was saved is questionable because of the high consumption on restarting, and there was the added wear on starters, plugs, batteries, and brakes.

Efforts at conservation of water were equally distressing. With newspapers, radio, and television belaboring all patriots to save water by every means possible, most toilets and lavatories in the hotels had chronic leaks and faucets were often left running. Chinese plumbers, equal to the worst in the world, were primarily at fault. However, the general populace never really supported conservation in their daily activities. They had grown impervious to the constant barrage of new slogans.

While planning appeared to be at a standstill at the CAAC, the U.S. domestic airline scene was in an upheaval. Braniff Airlines, eighth largest in terms of numbers of planes, had declared bankruptcy, dumping additional airplanes on an already weak market. A number of other airlines were deferring new airplane purchases, even declining to take delivery of some under firm contract.

With so many potential bargains available, the CAAC directed an increased attention to the need for expansion of their 747 fleet. Undelivered to Braniff were two 747-200 airplanes and one 747SP—all new—parked at the Boeing Wichita Kansas plant, awaiting resale.

Boeing, anxious to make the initial sale of 737-200 airplanes to the CAAC, viewed the Braniff machines as a bargaining chip in increasing the number of 737s that the Chinese would buy, and thus extended very attractive terms. As a result, Boeing made a proposal that tied these terms to the purchase of a minimum of ten 737 airplanes.

Secondly, Boeing offered additional concessions in training, spare parts, and other goods and services. The Chinese decided to purchase two additional 747s, but were having difficulty choosing between the 747-200, a 400+ passenger airplane, and the 300-passenger 747SP. Further, in the badly depressed market of 1982, many airlines were reducing their fleets, offering one or two airplanes at bargain prices. The CAAC claimed to have a total of 49 offers, including L-1011s and DC-10s.

With Lockheed having announced that the Tristar line was being closed, the L-1011 became a closeout sale. Of course, buyers could expect to be on their own after the sale, with reduced support and long lead times for spare parts. The L-1011 and the DC-10 were also the wrong airplanes for the Chinese, who required four-engined airplanes for the long Pacific runs and twins for the domestic service.

Nevertheless, all those offers were heady stuff for the overworked CAAC staff. They continued sorting the marbles and deliberating, aware that they were enjoying the strongest buyer's market in a decade—but oblivious to the serious erosion in their own progress.

A parade of Boeing officials came to Beijing during the summer of 1982, and ultimately the president of the Boeing

Commercial Airplane Company made a final offer—one that he was prepared to turn his back to. The Chinese had not budged an inch from the year earlier position of what they were willing to pay, while Boeing had continued to improve the terms all through the year. At the final meeting, the Chinese director of finance likened the negotiations to a 1,000-meter race. He said Boeing had already run the first 900 meters and now only needed to run the last 100 to close the deal. He refused to believe that Boeing had in fact delivered its rock-bottom offer.

It was the final offer, and the terms were unambigious. The proposal stated that the price and delivery conditions were good until the 30th of September 1982, "subject to prior sale." Similar terms had been offered to other airlines for the identical airplanes. The hazard of the planes' being lost to the Chinese was increasing daily.

On September 13, a fateful day for the CAAC planners, the Boeing sales director notified them that another airline had accepted the Boeing proposal and only needed to make a down payment to close the deal. He also phoned me from the United States and urged that I speak to the CAAC officials personally to make them understand that we were not merely engaging in sales posturing. At the time, unknown to Boeing, the Chinese had decided to accept the proposal for the two 747-200 airplanes, tied to the purchase of the ten 737-200 machines, but were still playing coy on the last "100 meters."

The Chinese planning committee had recommended the 747-200, judging the SP to be the wrong buy since they already had three and believed the next increment should be the larger-capacity airplane. However, they firmly believed the Boeing call was merely additional sales pressure.

When I spoke to Mr. Xu Zhengle, the deputy general manager of their procurement arm, he said he understood, and would immediately discuss our concerns with the director of finance.

"Mr. Xu," I cautioned, "as soon as the other airline sends in the deposit, the airplanes will be gone."

"Well, we are planning to have a reply to your proposal on the 25th. You know it doesn't expire until the 30th."

"That doesn't make any difference. The clause stipulates the date of expiration is subject to prior sale."

"We'll try to move fast, probably by the first of next week."

"That may be too late, Mr. Xu."

The week passed. I did not follow up, afraid of being too pushy, creating the wrong effect, especially in the event that the other airline failed to put up the money. On the following Sunday, the 19th of September, I was awakened from a sound sleep with the news. The other airline had telexed a deposit. The airplanes were sold.

I found it difficult to sympathize with the Chinese. Like chess players, sometimes too intent on their own next move, they had been oblivious to the rest of the world, so taken with their own importance that they had wholly ignored the facts of the marketplace. They were devastated at the news. When I called Mr. Xu on Monday morning and informed him of the latest developments, I was greeted by a stunned silence. Finally recovering, as if to turn back the clock, he stammered, "But we sent in our acceptance telex this morning."

"I'm sorry, it appears you were about twenty-four hours too late."

After another long pause, Mr. Xu accepted the finality of the event. "But Boeing must have a remedy," he responded plaintively.

Privately feeling that the CAAC had lost the best deal ever offered in the history of the Boeing Company, I told him that the home plant was reviewing possibilities. Boeing came back with an attractive offer of one large airplane off the assembly line, for delivery in December 1983, and the CAAC breathed new life into their analysis of the utility of the fourth 747SP, so a deal was put together.

The experience helped negotiations all along the line. The Chinese had learned a lesson, and dealing would be more equitable in the future.

The purchase agreement for ten 737-200 airplanes was signed by the CAAC officials at 10:44 A.M. Beijing time, Saturday, November 6, 1982, fourteen months after the flight demonstration tour in China. The CAAC had still not realized the importance of improving their long-range planning cycle.

The new 737 airplanes were scheduled for assignment to the Guangzhou Region, the first three being delivered in February 1983. Later in November, the contracts were signed for the 747SP and the 747-200 Combi, a plane which the CAAC used to inaugurate combined cargo and passenger flights to the United States and Europe in January 1984. With the acquisition of the added long-range lift, the CAAC became competitive in both passenger and cargo markets anywhere in the world, a giant stride from their position in 1979. On the domestic front, there were more problems to be solved, but the purchase of the 737 airplanes represented a significant step in modernization of the fleet. Further, the Shanghai region of the CAAC, taking a different approach on new equipment, took delivery of two new McDonnell Douglas MD-82 airplanes in December 1983.

The Guangzhou region was inadequately staffed, poorly equipped, and lacked the fixed facilities to handle modern jet airplanes. Boeing stationed four field representatives there and provided extensive support in spares planning, flight and maintenance training.

On another related front, the CAAC was also making progress. In October 1981 they had screened their mechanics staff to find the ones most capable in the use of the English language. Choosing fourteen candidates, they sent them to an English polishing school in Tianjin for six months. The fourteen students were then enrolled in the Spartan School of Aviation in Tulsa, Oklahoma, with the goal of obtaining Airframe and Powerplant (A&P) licenses. Although two were dropped because of their inadequate grasp of English, by November 1982 the two top students had returned to China, proud owners of their full A&P licenses.

The following February the remaining ten returned to Beijing, eight having been awarded full licenses and two, partials. The new licensed mechanics represented the first step in the CAAC goal of having the Beijing maintenance base certified under the FAA of the United States. Based on my discussions with the chief translator, Mr. Zhang, the day was probably five years away, but the Chinese continued to pursue it in their tenacious, patient way.

Acquisition of the A&P licenses brought to the surface a Chinese trait that I had long since discovered and that influenced my assessment that a technologically competent China was more a matter of generations than merely the passing of a few years.

Theoretically, those mechanics who had earned the license were capable of understanding the complex systems of Western airplanes and engines, reading and interpreting the Boeing maintenance and dispatch manuals, adept at the use of tools, and above all could troubleshoot malfunctions and reach logical decisions as to the cause, effect, and remedy. Thus, it should have been possible to designate any one of them to go to a remote base such as Shanghai, Guangzhou, or Tianjin, and to operate independently on the routine dispatch of airplanes.

However, in the real world of China, things did not work that way. When told that they were now fully qualified to handle a 747, they shrank from accepting the role, responding that they did not have sufficient experience. They were reluctant, even fearful, of taking such responsibility. That reluctance was deeply rooted in the age-old practice of taking directions but not assuming responsibility. There had always been a boss to report to—who would be responsible. Individual responsibility and initiative, which is routinely accepted in Western countries, was a foreign notion.

On still another front, as a condition of the sale of the 737/747 package, Boeing agreed to increase support of the fledgling aircraft manufacturing industry in China. The agreement with CATIC was fully implemented, and the first parts machined at the Xian Aircraft Factory were shipped to Boeing in December 1982. Boeing had also agreed to increase the amount and complexity of work in the factory, and in the summer of 1983 a contract was discussed for the manufacture of complete 737-300 vertical fins. The contract was finally signed in April 1984, an important milestone, with delivery of the first vertical fin visualized as early as mid-1988.

If we assume that those milestones were achieved, that the Chinese funded and outfitted their factory with the proper tooling and equipment, and trained sufficient people in engineering, manufacturing, tooling, and quality control, it is entirely conceivable that they could build a complete airplane capable of meeting Western standards before the turn of the century.

In February 1983 I traveled to Guangzhou to join the CAAC in welcoming the first two of the Little Giants, as the 737s were nicknamed, which arrived twenty-four minutes apart on February 14th. After Boeing flight instructors completed the training of Chinese crews on site in Guangzhou, regular service was initiated on April 1, 1983, from Guangzhou to Hong Kong. A few days later, 737 flights were joining Guangzhou with the tourist center of Guilin.

By the end of 1983 five airplanes had been delivered, and their service was rapidly expanding throughout the southeastern CAAC system.

As if to pinpoint the paucity of technological infrastructure in China, it was soon determined that the airplanes were unable to make radio contact with some of the ground stations operating on a frequency range whose maximum would not reach the minimum of the airplane transmitter.

CHAPTER 19

AIRPLANE ACQUISITIONS, hotel construction, and hordes of tourists notwithstanding, 1982 was a year of testing for China. For the CAAC it was a year that they might prefer to forget. In April, a Trident bound for Guilin crashed into a mountain, killing all 112 passengers on board. According to one source,[1] a casually spoken "OK" by the control tower in the Guilin airport caused the airplane to lower its altitude prematurely. Chinese authorities have continued to maintain nearly total silence on the cause of the crash, but did announce that air crews would be given additional instructions on safe operation.

Three months later, on July 25, five hijackers seized a Chinese airliner on a domestic flight from Xian to Shanghai, demanding that it be flown to Taiwan via Hong Kong. The captain pretended to agree but flew around Shanghai for two and one-half hours. With the four-engine IL-18 running low on fuel and members of the crew and passengers engaged in a bloody battle with the hijackers inside the aircraft, the plane managed to land at the Shanghai airport, but not before a bomb planted in the right-hand forward lavatory exploded, blowing a hole in the fuselage. The hijackers were overcome by the crew, aided by passengers wielding umbrellas, bottles, and mops, and finally collapsed on the floor of the aircraft, in a pool of

[1] *South China Morning Post*, February 3, 1983.

blood, unconscious, later to be dragged off by the heels to waiting authorities.

In accordance with Chinese criminal law, the five were put on trial, sentenced to death, and deprived of their political rights. After being pronounced guilty, they appealed to the Higher People's Court, which upheld the sentence. The Supreme People's Court confirmed the death sentence, and the hijackers were executed on August 19, a swift justice that sent a powerful message to anyone contemplating a similar crime.

Misfortune continued to dog the airline, and on Christmas Eve 23 people died and 30 were injured when another IL-18 caught fire moments before the plane was forced to land at Guangzhou. The CAAC officials were bombarded with a barrage of criticism. One report indicated that the fire trucks at the airport were unable to fight the blaze because their water tanks were empty.[2]

Robert Scott, of the International Federation of Airline Pilots Association, was especially critical. "I am very disturbed by what appears to be slack security, outmoded equipment, and inappropriate training by CAAC," he said.[3] "The Chinese are making fairly significant steps to improve their standards," Scott continued, "but they were so far behind in the first place that it's going to take some time before satisfactory levels are reached."

Perhaps the most serious criticism was that political considerations apparently outweighed those of safety, at least in the case of the hijacking. Scott noted, "On almost any other airline, standard procedure would be to get the airplane on the ground to increase the chance of survival."[4]

One Western diplomat based in Beijing remarked, "It seems

[2] UPI, *Japan Times,* May 30, 1983.
[3] *Newsweek,* January 24, 1983.
[4] *Ibid.*

that the Chinese are fully prepared to let one of their craft go down with all hands on board rather than permit it to land in Taiwan."

From a financial point of view, the CAAC airline was doing well. Profits were in the $75-million range for 1982, an increase of 20 percent over 1981. By 1984 they had grown to $112 million.[5]

The organizational structure of the airline posed serious problems for its ability to improve quickly. Internally, quality control was not an independent organization, and there was no separate regulatory body outside the airline similar to the FAA in the United States. The CAAC made its own regulations and policed itself. Their organization would require a complete overhaul before they could hope to qualify as a foreign FAA-approved repair station.

In Beijing certain foreign experts were doing some sloganeering of their own. One executive claimed the airline was suffering from the "Three N's" no information, no motivation, and no competition.

Misery and misfortune were no respecters of calendars, and continued into 1983. In May a Trident, hijacked on a flight from Shenyang in northeastern China to Shanghai, was forced to land at a small airfield outside Seoul, South Korea. That incident triggered a full-scale attack on the CAAC management by the press. Reacting both to public opinion and the increasing fears that eventually hijackers would succeed in diverting planes to Taiwan, the authorities ordered a nationwide crackdown on domestic travel rules.

As a starter, 25 percent of all domestic flights were cancelled. Permission to fly, a routine requirement for every Chinese national, was severely tightened, with all peasants

---

[5] *China Daily,* November 29, 1983; *Air Transport World,* May 1985.

and lesser workers summarily forbidden, and middle-level workers were ordered to obtain approval at a much higher level than before. These measures were kept in force until a modern set of security equipment could be put in place at all domestic airports.

If the airline was having its image bruised and battered, and was looking for calmer waters ahead, the nation, too, took sobering stock of itself during 1982, which was known as the year of the census. In July the census was taken on a nationwide basis, the third since the liberation, the most recent count dating back to 1964. To tabulate the figures, the Chinese used 29 computers, 8 of which were produced locally and 21 bought from IBM with the help of a $15.6-million grant from the United Nations. The 1964 census had been entirely compiled with the abacus. The final count of the 29 provinces, municipalities, and autonomous regions on the mainland, including the 4.23 million persons in the armed forces, came to 1,008,175,288, up 313,593,529 since 1964, an annual growth rate of 2.1 percent. The proportion of males to females was 106.3 to 100.

The stark, unyielding numbers sobered even the most optimistic of those responsible for population control. With the goal of not exceeding 1.2 billion by the turn of the century, and then a gradual reduction, an annual growth rate of 0.95 percent had to be maintained. The State Council's census group and the State Statistical Bureau, in studying the trends, commented that the goal presented a very difficult task.

The population of cities and towns was pegged at 206,588,582, leaving 800 million in the countryside. The population of Shanghai, the largest city, was 11,859,748; Beijing, the capital and second largest, 9,230,687; and Tianjin, third largest, 7,764,151—all figures including the suburbs. However in 1983, Chongqing, by annexing many small towns, claimed to have surpassed Shanghai.

The census also revealed the following:

> Illiterates and semi-illiterates (people twelve years old and above who cannot read or can read only a few words) numbered 235,820,000—23.4 percent, or nearly one-fourth of the population. Progress was noted when these figures were compared to the 1964 census, which showed 38.1 percent in the illiterate and semi-illiterate category.
>
> Of the total population, 4,414,495 had attained university degrees and 1,602,474 were undergraduates, including both those who studied previously and those now attending the university. In comparison with other countries of the world: for every 10,000 people there were 11.6 university students in China. India had 58.4, the Soviet Union 106, Japan 210, and the United Stated 507.
>
> China was far down the list—third lowest in the world—in terms of the average amount spent on education per person. It was one of the few that did not have compulsory education.

Many leaders were still reluctant to spend money on education, while at the same time they were blindly expanding capital construction. Nevertheless, delegates to the Sixth National People's Congress in June 1983 reported that great progress had been made in the last two years, citing the example of Beijing. There, two years previously, 80 percent of the 3 million workers and employees had an education below the level of middle-school student. But in the next two years several thousand evening and spare-time training schools had been established and attended by more than 1 million people.

The Chinese claimed that 93 percent of primary-school-age children in the cities and towns and 92 percent of those in rural areas were enrolled in schools in 1983.[6] In the best pre-liber-

---

[6] *Ibid.*, October 28, 1982; July 4, 1983.

ation year, approximately 20 percent of eligible children were enrolled in primary schools, leaving 80 percent to grow up illiterate.[7]

The drop-out rate continued to be high because of the financial situation of families or the need for more helping hands on the farms. Paradoxically, the increased affluence on the farms was leading parents to keep their children home to work in the fields.

A significant milestone was reached on May 27, 1983, when in Beijing, Ph.D.s were awarded to eighteen postgraduate students, marking the first time in Chinese history that Ph.D.s have been awarded to students trained under Chinese educators.[8]

From the beginning of normalization, the tourist gates strained to handle the potential. There was an inadequacy of hotels, transport, and communication. By 1982 the flow had reached the awkward stage wherein new initiatives were required if the Western tourist traffic was to continue to grow. Thus, in 1982, China took new steps to facilitate tourism.

In the fall of 1982, the National Tourism Administration directed that it was no longer necessary for tourists to come in groups—individuals would be accepted. Up to that point, essentially all tourists traveled in groups, their itineraries worked out by the official travel agency. Very little choice, if any, was available to cater to individual desires. Mr. Han Kehua, director of the National Tourism Administration, announced at the tourism conference in October 1982 in Beijing that the goal was for individuals to comprise 20 to 30 percent of all tourists by 1990 and 30 to 40 percent by the end of the century.

[7] *Ibid.*, March 5, 1983.
[8] *Ibid.*, May 28, 1983.

Concurrent with the liberalization of travel policies for entrance to the country, the Ministry of Public Security revealed a major improvement in freedom of movement within China. Henceforth, they directed, permission would no longer be necessary to travel to 29 principal cities. Even the more remote areas, and China has many, were beginning to open. In 1983 two of the most inaccessible provinces—Qinghai in Central Asia, and Ningxiahui, a mainly Moslem region in the northwest—were opened to foreign travelers.

These measures were only a beginning. On February 15, 1985, 67 cities and towns were added to the free-access list. The overall total, including areas where permits would be available, reached 257.[9]

The Tourism Conference of 1982 reviewed the many serious bottlenecks that existed in the improvement of the environment for tourists. Although hotel accommodations and transportation were cited as most worrisome, the quality of service still lagged far behind international standards.

For individuals, it was still nearly impossible to plan and secure an itinerary that would remain glued together. It was necessary for a person to wait until reaching the first destination before booking onward, or even making a hotel reservation in advance.

In October 1982 Frank Ching[10] presented some homely examples and insight to the state of affairs in the tourist industry. "One group bound for Peking was told in mid-air that the destination had been changed to Xian, while they waited for hotel rooms to open up in the Chinese capital. Then they had to return to Xian for another visit, since that was what the itinerary originally demanded.

"When China first opened up to tourists, the novelty was

---

[9]*Ibid.*, February 15, 1985.
[10]*Asian Wall Street Journal,* October 28, 1982.

sufficient for many people to be willing to put up with dirty bathrooms, inadequate lighting, surly waiters, and high prices. Now, if China wants to continue to attract increasing numbers of tourists, it will have to change deeply ingrained attitudes that result in regulations that appear designed for the convenience of roomboys, waiters, and other 'service personnel' rather than for hotel and restaurant patrons.

"The Park Hotel in Shanghai had been renovated and now boasts airconditioning, an amenity that wasn't available when this visitor first stayed there in 1973. Earlier this month, however, when Shanghai was still hot, the hotel's central airconditioning had already been turned off. A request to the front desk for the airconditioning to be turned back on elicited the remark: 'In all my years here, I've never met a hotel guest like you.'

"An individual tourist's travails in China can easily start with officious customs officials at the Peking airport. There are usually two lines for baggage inspection and, recently, a returning foreign resident headed for the shorter line, but was waved away and told to stand in the longer line. Asked for the reason, the customs officer said, "Because I say so. In our country, each person has to obey and go wherever he is assigned."

The airconditioning situation that Ching discusses in Shanghai was not unusual. In nearly every area where a utility was involved, a set of rigid rules existed for its use. Service personnel, and even managers, had no authority to deviate. In Beijing, the edict which regulated the utilization of coal stoves was only a small part of the maze of directives that were in effect.

In the Beijing Hotel, Beijing's showplace hostelry, heat, airconditioning, light, and water supplies were all furnished and controlled by an inviolate set of rules. Every spring I wrote several letters of complaint about hot rooms, to no avail. When the airconditioning was finally turned on, on the appointed day, central control would turn it off from midnight to 4:00 A.M. to save electricity. The Chinese, with their inimitable logic, perceived no reason to have the airconditioning on while the guests were sleeping, believing they would not know the difference. When approached about this curious practice, the manager would shrug defensively and say: "But many guests don't like it so cold when they sleep"—this in spite of the fact that each room had a switch to turn off the airconditioning locally.

By the end of 1984, with five years of experience, I was more convinced than ever that the gap that China had to close was generational. Even after the new freedoms to travel within China had been promulgated, only the slightest straying from the beaten paths between the largest cities resulted in frustrating and disappointing experiences.

In November Beth and I decided to test the purely local travel as individuals, using the trains. Having heard that there were some very interesting statues and carvings in the limestone cliffs at a city called Datong, about 200 miles west of Beijing in Shanxi Province, an eight-hour trip, we decided to take the 10:45 P.M. Friday evening train.

Datong, although close to Beijing, was not one of the 29 cities to be taken off the restricted list. We still required a travel permit. Thus, via my interpreter, I set in motion the bureaucractic machinery necessary to make the visit a reality. First, a trip to the Public Safety Bureau was required to apply for a permit. That involved leaving our passports and residence books at the Bureau for twenty-four hours. A second trip was required to retrieve them.

Next, we went to the China Travel Bureau to order the tickets. This step required three trips. We were allowed to purchase a ticket for one way only. The officials insisted that we must buy our return ticket after arrival in Datong. A second trip was required to pick up the tickets, and a third to arrange with the Travel Bureau for a taxi and an interpreter in Datong. It was not possible to combine all those items in one visit, since everything had to be done step-wise, one step at a time.

There were two return trains, one at noon and one at night. We decided to try for the noon train, since we would arrive in Datong at 6:45 A.M., have breakfast, spend two hours at the caves, return to the station, and take the noon train back to Beijing. "Not possible to make reservations," they said. When I offered to pay extra, they demanded a letter from my "unit chief," requesting the noon train from Datong. The train came in from farther west, we were told, and thus very few passengers could be taken at Datong.

"Why do I need to make still another trip to this office with a letter?" I complained. "I am my own unit chief. I will write the letter."

Whereupon I took a sheet of paper from my notebook and proceeded to write a guarantee for full round-trip payment in the event that we failed to appear for the noon train in Datong. The officials stared—incredulous.

Suffice it to say that on November 12, 1982, we arrived at the Peking Railroad Station in Beijing, and the "soft sleeper" berths we had purchased were ready. They were facing, transverse, double bunks. Fortunately, we were the only two in the four-place compartment. Pure, unplanned, good fortune.

Chinese train officials go to great lengths to assure arrival exactly on the appointed hour, allowing ample time in the schedule to handle any conceivable delay, i.e., eight hours to travel 200 miles—often pulling on to a siding to wait when ahead of schedule.

Datong, at an elevation of 2,500 feet and located at the same 40-degree north latitude as Beijing, was already bitter cold. The temperature struggled up from 15 degrees F. in the early morning to a high of 38 degrees during the day.

Carrying our toast and hard-boiled eggs with us, we had breakfast on the train and upon arrival were ready to go straight to the Travel Agency to acquire our return tickets. "Impossible," announced our guide, without blinking an eye or checking with anyone. "All full." Thus, in spite of my official letter of guarantee and the payment of ten yuan for a telephone call to make the reservations, we had nothing.

We resigned ourselves to the situation, slowed down our internal clocks, and searched for a warm place out of the bitter wind where we could wait while our interpreter secured the tickets for the night train.

A primitive city of nearly 1 million, Datong is situated in the middle of one of the largest coal deposits in China. With 2.4 billion tons of proved reserves, Shanxi Province was expected to figure prominently in China's energy development program. In fact, in March 1983, Occidental Petroleum signed an agreement[11] with China to develop and operate jointly an open pit mine. The project rated as the most ambitious joint venture since China opened its doors to foreign investment in 1979. The final contract was signed on June 28, 1985.[12]

Occidental is expected to invest $230 million for equipment and personnel, and officials estimate, based on going prices, that the project should produce annual revenues of $600 to $750 million while recovering 15 million tons of coal the first year. The region has the annual potential of tripling first-year output.

Our visit was strictly for sightseeing, and we thoroughly enjoyed our tour through the limestone cliffs, marveling at the ancient carvings. However, even though the artifacts may rate high in the hierarchy of things to see in China, tourism to

---

[11] *International Herald Tribune,* March 9, 1983.
[12] *China Daily,* July 1, 1985.

Datong will remain a trickle unless the transportation system is completely overhauled. Datong had no airport, and we could attest that the train trip was for the hardy adventurer rather than for the average tourist. Our return trip on the train was more spartan still. Having been denied the noon train, we watched while our promised evening train went through without stopping. "Completely full," we were told. However, by a happy coincidence, a special midnight train was coming in from the west, and we could board.

Stumbling through the dark passageways behind the conductor, who blinked a pale flashlight every few seconds, we were ushered into a compartment that the attendant unlocked from the outside. We heard snoring in the blackness of the interior. Striking a match, I discovered that two beds were already occupied in the four-berth compartment—two middle-aged Chinese men. Beth and I undressed in the dark, crawled into our bunks, and slept fitfully for the eight-hour trip back to Beijing.

There are numerous tourist attractions in China on a similar scale with Datong, many of them still undeveloped and off the beaten path, putting a double challenge on the hotel builders and the transportation system.

In May 1983, China's GNP report indicated that the economy had grown 9 percent in 1982. However, in many ways the Chinese considered that 1982 contained some serious ills and bad portents. The results of the new liberalizations were beginning to be felt. The central government had relinquished a significant amount of economic control to the localities.

The Chinese had been trying to hold down spending while concentrating their limited resources on the production of consumer goods. However, despite the efforts to slow the production of heavy industrial goods, production rose sharply, and investment on new projects was out of control. In releasing the final figures for 1982, the government communique was straightforward in voicing its displeasure. "The scale of capital construction was overextended and investment excessive," it read, a strong slap at the local cadres.

With so much preaching of reform by Deng and CCP Chairman Hu Yaobang, many of the past sins of the regime were becoming open sores, and threatening what the leadership sloganized into "Three Crises": no trust in the Party, no confidence in socialism, and no belief in Communism. Some of those on the far right were bold enough to call for a two-party system.

Those signals were sufficient for the government to crack down, and the pendulum began to swing back to stronger central control. The stage was set for the Sixth National People's Congress in June 1983, where Premier Zhao Ziyang told the inaugural session that recentralization was seen to be necessary to avert another squeeze on capital and resources such as that which caused the 1979–1981 economic readjustment.

Equally important were the political overtones. If targets were too high and not met, the political and economic impact would be unfavorable and would dampen the people's enthusiasm, thus upsetting the delicate balance of support that was so necessary.

CHAPTER 20

DETHRONING FALSE GODS and overcoming myths are herculean tasks in any society in any age. For China the double problem of demythologizing Mao without destroying the progress that his regime had brought at times seemed to defy solution. In 1983, seven years after the Cultural Revolution ended, the political trials of the radicals involved in that episode were concluded. During the trials, a methodical process of sloganizing and re-education was carried on gradually to mold public opinion to the new thinking.

Ending of the trials indicated that the "spring cleaning" of the minds of the Chinese had been completed, and the nation was considered receptive to the news that intellectuals were also workers, only of a different kind. A campaign to make them accepted again began in earnest.

In a report carried by the official press agency in June 1983, the President of the Supreme People's Court, Mr. Jiang Hua, said that 326,000 people who had been framed or falsely imprisoned during the chaotic decade had been exonerated after court review. The numbers included many of the moderate Communists who were running China under the modernization programs. Even Deng himself had once been accused of being the "number two capitalist roader."

Although there were many unrepentant radicals still in the Communist Party, it was necessary for the courts to take the first step to provide the legitimatizing therapy which could defuse or minimize the danger of a serious backlash to the leadership. With the courts officially declaring the completion of the political trials, Deng was on firm ground to go forward with the final phases of his house cleaning.

By 1983 it was possible openly to criticize the "leftist influences" in the various levels of the government, industry, and education. In fact, 1983 had suddenly become the "year of the intellectuals." Mr. Zhao Ziyang himself put the final stamp of approval on the new treatment of intellectuals in his address to the First Session of the Sixth National People's Congress on June 6, 1983.[1]

"To win honor for the socialist motherland and contribute one's share to its socialist modernization has become the watchword of our time. We have in recent years properly solved a series of problems left over from the past. We examined large numbers of cases involving unjust, false, and wrong charges and reversed the verdicts that had been passed on them. People who had been wrongly labelled bourgeois rightists received redress, as did small tradespeople, pedlars, rich peasants, counterrevolutionaries and bad elements who had become law-abiding working people through remoulding have had their designations removed, and large numbers of former Kuomintang Party, government and army personnel, and special agents were released from prison in conformity with our policy of leniency.

"Our struggle against serious crimes in the economic and other fields has helped ensure the socialist character and orientation of our efforts in various spheres of national construction. Although some destablilzing factors still exist in our society, which we must make continued efforts to eliminate, people have every reason to believe that the present situation of stability and unity is irreversible and that our great moth-

---

[1] *China Daily*, June 24, 1983.

erland will enjoy a long period of order and stability. No force on earth can hold back or undermine this historical trend."

The stage was set for a continued pressure to purge the leftist members of the Communist Party. It had become possible to criticize publicly those who blindly supported the "Two Whatevers": whatever Mao Zedong did *in* his lifetime, and whatever he said was correct.

Indeed, it was disclosed that Deng himself had criticized the "Two Whatevers" in an unpublished speech in 1977. Those criticisms have now been made public in a new book[2] that edit more than 400 of Deng's speeches, including 39 that were published for the first time. The obvious timing of Deng's works were fully to legitimatize the modernization policies and to solidify public support of the final purge of the remaining recalcitrant leftists.

Deng's thoughts as expressed in the book reflect the nation's experience; wrestling with the "leftists," rectifying past errors, and, finally, concentrating on modernization efforts.

In 1983, economic theorists, feeling the new freedoms of intellectual expression, were beginning to be heard from. In an editorial that would have cast the author in chains a few years before, and amazing for its candor, the views of Qian Jiaju, a Chinese economist, were summarized in four main points for the improvement of economic results:[3]

> *Economy in production.* "We have emphasized economy all along, but, ordinarily, only of consumer goods. We have neglected the most basic form, economy in production. I have visited factories in 19 provinces and municipalities since 1980 and have seen alarming waste in production.
>
> "We have called the United States a wasteful country. This is lopsided. While waste of consumer goods in America is

[2] "Selected Works of Deng Xiaoping," *China Daily,* July 1, 1983.
[3] *China Daily,* June 30, 1983.

really enormous, America, like most capitalist countries, pays much attention to economy in production. China, on the contrary, stresses economy in consumer goods and pays no heed to economy in production. This is putting first things last and works against improvement in economic results.''

The law of value. "We will have to understand the law of value before we can make the best use of it. The fact that we did not make good use of it in the past affects our ability to improve economic results now. Prices are absurd. They represent neither value nor the price of production as outlined by Karl Marx's theory (i.e., cost of production plus average profit). Prices have nothing to do with value, and value of production, profits, and production targets cannot explain economic results.

"The price of coal is much lower than its cost of production, which discourages increased production, and economical use of energy.

"High prices and large profits are likewise not advantageous to production. For example, the cost of making wristwatches is very low, but they sell for extraordinarily high prices. As a result, some watch factories make a profit despite poor management and low productivity."

The "communal pot" and "iron rice bowl." "Allocation of labor is centralized in the hands of labor departments, which assign workers and fix norms for wages. There is no free movement of personnel. Enterprises do not have the right to select or reject personnel. In many enterprises, it does not matter whether the worker is diligent or does no work at all. It is certainly a distortion to say that such egalitarianism is 'socialist superiority.' ''

Remnants of leftist thinking. "Leftism still dominates the thinking of many of our cadres, who strive for fake reputations and do not emphasize real benefits. They regard only value, quantity, and speed of production as important targets for evaluating the development of the economy. But economic laws are cruel. They will not give way to subjective wishes of men.''

Beginning in early 1983, and continuing up to the Sixth Congress in June, a literal flood of statements of support for the intellectuals appeared in the official Chinese press. In a meeting commemorating the centenary of the death of Karl Marx, Hu Yaobang said: "Knowledge and the intellectuals were necessary for overthrowing the old world, and they are even more important for building the new. Furthermore, in a country like China, with its low economic and cultural level, whether or not we are able to master modern science and culture is a pivotal factor determining success or failure in our contribution."[4]

Intellectuals had finally been accepted as workers, only of a different nature. In an editorial in early 1983, *China Daily* stated, "To trust in and take good care of intellectuals and to promote the virtuous, talented, and younger ones is only compatible with the interests of workers, peasants, and the whole nation."

Nevertheless, the Chinese found that merely recognizing, sloganizing, and accepting intellectuals on an official level was insufficient. The deep-seated mistrust that was the official party line for decades, in fact since the Republic was declared, would be hard to eradicate—another reminder that modernization was a generational metamorphosis.

The difficulties were expressed by Wang Zhiyu,[5] an official of the personnel department of the Ministry of Commerce, in commenting on the need to reform the work of personnel departments when carrying out the Party policy toward intellectuals. "It is true our cadres have achieved some improvement and made some reforms in their attitudes toward intellectuals," he said. "However, these reforms and methods are often marred by some cadres' hesitancy and indecisiveness in taking action.

"Some cadres give verbal acknowledgment of the importance of intellectuals, but deep in their hearts they still feel

[4] *Ibid.*, March 29, 1983.
[5] *China Daily,* March 17, 1983.

strongly that they are 'praised too highly,' still believing that they themselves should be in the more prominent place."

Wang also mentioned the condescending attitude that prevailed in many instances: "You must obey whatever I say" or "Do as the Party orders." He noted that the major reason for the wrong attitude of the cadres toward intellectuals was that the leftist ideas remaining since 1957 had not been entirely eradicated.

"Reform in terms of changing cadres attitudes toward intellectuals is now a 'must,' " Wang continued. "Intellectuals are indispensable to the nation's drive for modernization, and our cadres' concern for them must not remain only verbal. Some technical personnel could be promoted to leading positions where they can in turn promote others according to need."

The new realism began slowly to creep beyond sloganizing. Differentiation in pay scales, commensurate with educational level, was finally accepted as a necessary incentive for healthy growth, and regulations to make this a reality were set forth by the State in 1983.[6]

Party leader Deng Xiaoping was quick to point out shortcomings in the progress of the Chinese, not content to paper over deficiencies. This pragmatism began to rub off on successive layers of the bureaucracy, a fact that bodes well for the success of the current drive as the major turn-around in recent Chinese history.

Deng, in his "Selected Works," states, "China has been outdistanced in science and technology by the developed countries for 20 years."[7]

In his conversation with two leading members of the Party's Central Committee in May 1977, Deng pointed out that China had only 200,000 scientists and technicians, as opposed to the

---

[6]*Ibid.*, May 31, 1983.
[7]*Ibid.*, June 22, 1983.

1.2 million in the United States and 900,000 in the Soviet Union. More significantly, Deng added, "And the 200,000 include many aged, sick, or handicapped people, so the number of those who can play a useful role is even smaller."

The paucity of scientific brainpower can be graphically illustrated by a geometric model wherein, if the 1 billion people were represented by a 10-inch diameter sphere, the veneer of highly technologically trained would be equivalent to a single coat of lacquer on its surface.

Deng cited the example of Japan's Meiji Reform, which began in the late 1860s with particular emphasis on science and education. "The Meiji Reform was a modernization drive initiated by the emerging bourgeoisie. If they succeeded then, we proletariats should be able to do better now."

Education was one of the most talked-about subjects at the Sixth National People's Congress in June 1983. Deng summarized his opinions on education, saying, "The key to China's four modernizations is technical knowhow, and technical manpower development is one of the major projects in which we are going to invest."

Deng's selected works will not only have a lasting historical significance, but will very likely remain as a guide to China's socialist modernization.

The year 1983 was also the year of naysayers in the foreign press. Having become numbed by the excesses, reverses, and false starts under the Mao regime, the press did not take the new modernization seriously. Sol Sanders in May 1983[8] epitomized these negative thoughts, painting the Chinese efforts as another "Great Leap Nowhere." Pointing out the dichotomy in the new pragmatism as embodied in Hu Yaobang's declaration marking the centenary of Karl Marx death, where, after referring to the disastrous decade of the Cultural Revo-

---

[8] *Business Week,* May 23, 1983.

lution, he stated, "We have re-embarked on the road of integrating the universal truth of Marxism with the actual realities in China under the new historical conditions," Sanders suggested that his statement "flies in the face of reality."

The CCP released a resolution calling for the GNP of 2.8 trillion yuan ($1.4 trillion at official 1983 rates of exchange) by the year 2000, or over $1,000 per capita for the projected 1.2 billion Chinese. The claim was based on China's industrial growth, which averaged 8.1 percent from 1953 to 1981. The CCP document pointed out that the Soviet GNP rose at a rate of 7.5 percent between 1965 and 1975 and that Japan's GNP more than doubled from 1957 to 1970.

The article criticized the comparison, saying that it ignored the fact that the Soviets had a much broader economic foundation than China and the Japanese had an educational structure complemented by modern business management.

One cannot argue with the correctness of these facts. However, there is the inference that a failure by China to quadruple its GNP by the year 2000 would somehow unhorse the leadership and send the country tailspinning into chaos. Not so! Deadlines and goals in China are no more than an advanced form of sloganeering. They are designed to stir the people into action and keep their eyes off daily problems and firmly fixed instead on the goals on the horizon. The leadership has always been adept at ascribing the "correct reasons" for something not happening according to plan, and Chinese minds are prepared to accept the logic.

The Chinese will take whatever measures are necessary to adjust to the dichotomy of pragmatic economic policies embracing the market forces of supply and demand, with the Marxism model. Over a period of two or three generations, Chinese thinking can be remolded to operate within the new realities of the marketplace.

Because of all the handicaps and hazards that must be overcome, there is no substitute for central control, no matter how difficult and stifling it seems. The stark facts of illiteracy, technological backwardness, infrastructural lack, and population pressure argue strongly for such a posture. Nevertheless, there will come a time when central control can safely be reduced. It was attempted in 1979, and by 1982 found to be premature. In late 1982 and early 1983 central control was gradually tightened once more. Then in 1984 a new cycle of relaxation was noted, this time going much farther than ever before, with apparent success. As the Chinese themselves will continue to caution, one must not be impatient or tolerate excessive patience at the risk of progress—three strides forward and two back.

The final key to success for the Chinese nation is easy to pinpoint: the control of population. Without control—and eventual reduction—all ventures toward reaching Western standards of technology, modernization, and economic and social betterment will be lost in the miseries of the advancing tide of hungry mouths and broken spirits. There is no doubt whatsoever that the Chinese realize this key concept and will take whatever measures that are required.

Amanda Bennett[9] chronicled these efforts: "Chinese officials are trying nearly everything. They dig deep into citizens' private lives to keep baby-making at a minimum. They make lists and set quotas. They threaten, cajole, harass, educate, and plead. They mobilize economic incentives and social pressure and, when all else fails, resort to coercion.

"Reminders of China's birth-control policy are all over the country. At times, red banners strung across roads in cities and towns proclaim the joys of family planning. Huge posters of smiling mothers holding one fat, happy girl child encourage parents to love their daughters and not hope for sons. You can

[9] *Asian Wall Street Journal,* July 6, 1983.

light your cigarettes with birth-control propaganda matches ('It is good to have only one child,' the boxes read), fan yourself with birth-control propaganda fans, and blow your nose in birth-control propaganda handkerchiefs, all handed out by the Family Planning Commission.''

It is true that birth control is working better in the cities, where more attention can be directed. ''The sky is high and the Emperor is far away.'' However, the national resolve is to control the birthrate at all costs. The measures needed to mete out the same degree of control in the countryside will be found.

China, slightly larger than the United States and ranked third in the world in size, has less than half the arable land, while supporting around four times the population. These are the irrefutable facts that China's leaders must face. With current food production balanced precariously against the population, and with the certainty that a geometric progression will overtake an arithmetic one, the rigid controls on births must be accepted as hard and bitter facts by every person living in China today.

We in the West may criticize abortions, arbitrary refusal of pleas by families seeking more than one child, and excesses such an infanticide among baby girls, which these measures may foster, but we must recognize that there is no other course.

Evidence that the strict measures are working is apparent in the latest figures.[10]

China's economic goals have also been derided through simplistic techniques such as looking at recent history. ''In the past 30 years, CCP economic plans have failed repeatedly—from the 1965 effort to 'surpass the scientific standard of the advanced nations in 12 years,' to the 1958 campaign to 'surpass England in 15 years,' to the 1978 plan to make 10 Da

---

[10] *China Daily,* April 9, 1985.

Qings (named after the supposedly efficient oil center), and a 1980 call to 'realize the mechanization of agriculture.' "[11]

It is difficult to argue with historical facts. Those facts remain. Nevertheless, it is no more difficult to believe that there is a time and a place for dramatic change—major deviations heralding historical landmarks. The time has come in the history of China, in its place and the history of nations, for such a change. The leadership now has firmly realized the nation's unique place in this history. Standing at the hinge of a better tomorrow and final chaos, China's leaders are determined to adhere to the new initiatives of the modernization program.

[11] *Business Week,* May 23, 1983.

CHAPTER 21

THE YEAR 1983 brought the modernization efforts that had been put in place in 1979 into sharp focus. With the removal of the stigma from the intellectuals, China had at last put its house in order for the drive toward excellence in industry and technology that the new regime had envisioned.

There is an old adage that one continually overestimates what can be accomplished in a single year and underestimates what can be done in five. By any measure, the progress that had been made in China in the five-year period from 1979–1983 was dramatic.

Throughout 1983 the government was able show gains at all levels of agriculture, industry, science, education, and social endeavors without any evidence of leftist counteraction. The overhauling of business and manufacturing organizations to improve productivity and efficiency received special attention.

In reviewing the goals for 1983, a senior official of the Party's Central Committee said that the most important task was to maintain high standards while stepping up the pace of top-level shakeup of enterprises.

"At the end of 1982," he said, "60 percent of the initial group of enterprises had completed the reorganization of their leadership. But half were not up to standard. There was no marked improvement in their work performance, and those enterprises need to be shaken up this year."

"Fifteen hundred out of the 2,300 major large and medium-sized enterprises had yet to be shaken up, or needed re-doing," he said.

The official pointed out that some departments and enterprises took a simplistic view in carrying out the shakeup. They merely retained those who did not exceed the age limit and incorporated a few technical personnel, without considering whether the new leadership line-up as a whole met the political, age, and educational criteria set by the Party.

He stressed that any new leadership must include qualified engineers, as well as good business managers and administrators. They must be career-minded and talented leaders ready to open up new frontiers in the modernization drive. He added that the Party branch organizations, personnel, and educational departments of the enterprises should also include young economists and technical personnel with a college education.

Of particular note was the candor with which he addressed what he considered as the root-cause of the reluctance to carry out the shakeup, the "remnant leftist influences," which must be "further erased."

The culmination of all the speech-making, sloganeering, and posturing of 1983 that welcomed the intellectuals back into the fold was the October 12 announcement by the Communist Party of an overall drive to rectify the Party's working style and to consolidate Party organizations over the following three years. This drive was seen as the final purge by Deng to remove the leftist radicals. In the process, to appease the hardliners, the far rightists or "liberals" also felt the purge.

The rectification drive was launched in 1984, with the aim to consolidate the Party's ties with the people and strengthen the Party as a core of leadership in the cause of socialist modernization.

The rectification program set the following tasks:[1]

> *Achieving ideological unity.* That is to correct all the erroneous "left" and "right" tendencies that run counter to the four basic principles and to the Party line mapped out by the third plenary session of the 11th Party Central Committee.
>
> The four basic principles are: adherence to the socialist road, the people's democratic dictatorship, leadership by the Communist Party of China, and Marxism-Leninism and Mao Zedong Thought.
>
> *Rectifying the Party style.* That is to promote the revolutionary spirit of serving people wholeheartedly, check acts of seeking personal gain on the strength of one's power and position, and combat bureaucratic attitudes.
>
> *Strengthening discipline.* That is to adhere to the Party's organizational principle of democratic centralism, oppose patriarchy, factionalism, anarchism, and liberalism and correct the ineptitude and laxity of the Party organizations.
>
> *Purifying the Party organizations.* That is to sort out elements who persistently oppose and harm the Party and expel them from the Party in accordance with the Party Constitution, especially three types of persons.
>
> The first type refers to those who during the "Cultural Revolution" closely followed Lin Biao, Jiang Qing, and company; formed factions and cliques; seized political power through "rebellion"; rose to high positions; and committed evil with serious consequences.
>
> The second type refers to those who in the "Cultural Revolution" vigorously publicized the reactionary ideology of the Lin Biao and Jiang Qing counterrevolutionary cliques; formed gangs for doing evil; and, since the downfall of the Gang of Four, have either overtly or covertly continued with factionalist activities.

[1] *China Daily,* October 13, 1983.

The third type refers to those who beat, smashed and looted during the "Cultural Revolution." In principle these three types of people should be expelled from the Party, except those who have mended their ways after a long period of examination.

The time was past when inefficient enterprises would be tolerated. In announcing the results of China's 1983 industrial output, Zhao Weichen, Vice-Minister of the State Economic Commission, admitted that the supply of energy and raw materials was tight. "To solve the problem, the State will first supply those enterprises with good economic results. Limited supply will be given to those producing poor-quality goods," he said. "Or they will be closed, merged, or shifted to other lines of production."[2]

The State intensified its policies of urging more attention to economic results during 1984, seeking ways to eliminate marginal producers, encourage efficient ones, and change consumer habits.

Under the leftist influence in the past years, any attention, no matter how slight it might be, paid to the quality of food and styles of clothing and furniture was considered the basis for severe criticism. As a result, encouragement of consumption was out of the question.

These long-held, erroneous ideas on consumption taught people to be very frugal, and reserves of agricultural products piled up in warehouses. An example was the continuous bumper crops of cotton in recent years, creating a surplus of textile products. However, the average annual consumption of textile fiber per capita in China was a little more than three kilograms, one-tenth the amount in the developed countries and less than half the world average.

On the other hand, Chinese consumers were maintaining a

---

[2]*Ibid.*, July 9, 1983.

high rate of saving. At the end of 1983, the urban and rural savings had reached more than 89 billion yuan, proof that there is great potential in people's purchasing power.[3]

The Chinese suddenly discovered in 1984 that the answer was to encourage consumption rather than to curtail production. Many economists have recently begun to emphasize this new "correct" position.

The wisdom of Deng's policies in promoting light industry for production of consumer goods was starkly evident in recent figures released by the Ministry of Light Industry. The man in the street and the peasant in the countryside are far better off than at any time in their history, insurance that the current policies will be supported and promoted.

Figure 1 compares the output of nine common consumer products for 1978 and 1983.[4]

With the return of the intellectuals, those who understand production and consumption are no longer afraid to speak up. During the extreme of the leftist influence, i.e., the Cultural Revolution, poverty was considered to be revolutionary and prosperity meant revisionism. Indeed, if one were to gain riches, it was axiomatic that others must become poor as a result. This obviously false premise has now been discarded.

Indeed, in a major departure from the Soviet-style planning that had been in effect since the founding of the PRC, China actually introduced capitalistic market philosophy in its urban economy, following the October 1984 meeting of the Communist Party Central Committee.[5]

The new measures will give greater independence to 1 million State-owned enterprises and make them compete for survival. In addition, the program will separate government func-

---

[3] *Ibid.*, August 29, 1984.
[4] *Ibid.*, August 24, 1984.
[5] *Ibid.*, October 22, 1984.

FIGURE 1
Growth of Consumer Items between 1978 and 1983

	Wrist-watches	Bicycles	Sewing Machines	Radios	Washing Machines	Refrigerators	TV Sets	Electric Fans	Cameras
Production in 1978	13.5 M	8.5 M	4.9 M	11.7 M			0.5 M		0.18 M
Production in 1983	34.7 M	27.6 M	10.9 M	19.9 M	3.7 M	0.19 M	6.8 M	10.5 M	0.93 M
Number owned by every 100 urban families (1983)	268	160	76	105	29	1.7	83	64	7.3

tions from purely economic functions, which will be left to plant managers, operating within guidelines. The decision will also mean that China will limit central planning, phase out extensive consumer subsidies, and leave prices of many products to be determined by supply and demand.

New emphasis is being placed on the importance of competition, the engine that drives capitalism. However, the Chinese continue to refer to this phenomenon as bringing into full play the superiority of the socialist system.

Pressure toward the new direction was felt by the CAAC management throughout 1983, but they failed to respond in a positive manner. Implementing only incremental change, CAAC's planning and organizational ability to step up to the massive undertaking of overhauling the domestic airline operations was falling short—actually lagging behind the required rate to keep abreast of the new waves of travelers who were being drawn to China by the expanding tourist sites and the completion of dozens of modern new hotels. At the highest levels of government, the CAAC was berated and warned to get its house in order—to complete internal shakeups commensurate with the demand for change. Convinced that this would not be done internally, the Central Government interceded actively to consider and promote joint ventures. In the spring of 1984, the government approved the formation of "independent" regional airlines in several provinces along the southeast coast, including Shanghai.[6] The goal was to introduce competition for the CAAC, the State-owned airline, and jar it out of the doldrums, eventually to provide service equivalent to airlines in the West.

With the handwriting on the wall, Mr. Shen Tu, director general of the CAAC, announced that the airline "had plans

---

[6] *Flight International*, 19 May, 1984. *China Daily*, May 23, 1984.

to expand the managerial powers of local aviation bureaus to allow them to become financially independent, responsible for their own accounting and management."[7] Thus the stage was set for the six regions of the CAAC gradually to evolve into separate domestic airlines, competing with each other on many routes.

Pressure for speed-up in the reorganization of China's airlines increased, and after a flurry of planning meetings a dramatic departure was announced in November, wherein the CAAC would completely disappear as an operating entity and would function only as a State Council department, handling administrative and regulatory duties. In its place would be created six separate airline companies, operating domestic and, in some cases, international services.[8]

The first three of these new companies, Air China, China Eastern Airways, and China Southern Airways, were formed in the first half of 1985. Initially, Beijing-based Air China will handle international flights and major domestic services. China Eastern Airways, based in Shanghai, will eventually be another new international airline; in its early stages, however, it will fly major domestic routes. The Guangzhou-based China Southern Airways will also concentrate on domestic service before going international. China Southwestern Airways, next to be formed, will be headquartered in Chengdu and will offer mainly domestic services. The far northwest and northeast regional companies will be formed last.

Local air companies will be set up in remote and border regions including Tibet, Xinjiang, and Inner Mongolia. They will provide inter-provincial services in cooperation with other companies. Preparations are also underway for the establishment of the China Capital Helicopter Company.

[7] *China Daily,* August 29, 1984.
[8] *China Daily,* November 3, 1984; February 6, 1985.

Local provincial governments are also being encouraged to buy aircraft, build airports, and set up joint air companies. China's first local air company, the Xiamen Company Ltd, was launched in Fujian Province early in 1984, eventually purchasing Boeing 737-200 airplanes.

The first of China's state agencies to be deregulated and carved up, the CAAC has been chosen by Deng Xiaoping as the model for dismantling other bureaucracies.[9]

Overall, no pumpkins will suddenly become beautiful carriages. Growth will evolve step-wise in the patient Chinese manner, but the clarion call to introduce market forces in the air transportation system of the country supplied early proof that deeds are replacing previously unrealized slogans.

During 1983 China's civil airplane manufacturing industry maintained slow but steady progress. The lessons learned from the unsuccessful Yun-10 project had been assimilated. Relegating the eventual production of larger sophisticated aircraft to the products of joint ventures with American firms, the Chinese concentrated on small and medium-sized planes. Five designs were completed and committed to production. They were the Yun-5 and Yun-11, small, multi-purpose transports; a medium-sized freighter, the Yun-8; a small helicopter, the Zhi-5; and the most advanced and largest of the group, a medium-sized passenger plane with 40 seats, the Yun-7.

Aircraft manufacturing is considered as the "flower of industry," reflecting the industrial level of a nation, and the Chinese are determined to reach parity with the West. Achievement of parity is proving to be elusive. The plan first to build small and medium airplanes and then expand to larger and more sophisticated machines is good in principle, but is progressing much more slowly than the Chinese planners had anticipated.

[9]*Business Week,* January 14, 1985.

At Xian, where the Antonov 24, a Russian look-alike of the Fairchild F-27, was being copied by the Chinese as the Yun-7, results were disappointing. Production had been approved in early 1982, prompting the CAAC to purchase 15 of the machines. However, when trial service began in 1984, performance was far short of expectations. The airplane was heavier than its clone and exhibited inferior workmanship, which caused the CAAC to lose interest in further purchases, even considering refusal to take delivery of the first full increment. Reaching for a remedy, the Xian Aircraft Company invited Boeing to review the design and manufacturing methods, with the goal of improving the performance of the aircraft.

The Xian experience, following on the heels of the Yun-10 failure, nudged the Chinese to more serious consideration of a joint manufacturing venture with a United States firm, and early in 1984 the Shanghai Industrial Corporation signed a letter of intent with McDonnell Douglas to assemble 25 MD-82 twinjets in the Shanghai factory. A request to Boeing to offer a proposal for co-production quickly followed, and in the summer of 1984 a letter of intent was signed for a similar program involving 25 to 40 model 737-300 airplanes. In April 1985, the Chinese announced the signing of a contract with McDonnell Douglas for co-production of 25 MD-82s at the Shanghai Aircraft Factory, birthplace of the illfated Y-10.

Considering China's urgent need for medium-range airplanes in large numbers, and the emphasis on airline growth as a linchpin of the industrial modernization program, it is easily conceivable that a Boeing co-production program will also receive a go-ahead at the Xian Aircraft Factory in the future. Beyond simply providing airplanes, such a step would introduce direct competition into Chinese industry, a long-sought goal of Deng Xiaoping.

During the same period of accelerated activity in 1985, the Chinese also announced the purchase of British BAC-146 and

Russian TU-154 short-range airplanes, as well as, Airbus A310s, Boeing 767s and 737-300s, Boeing's latest design.

Proving that the shakeup in the CAAC was no tentative move, Shen Tu, a political figure, was replaced as Director General in April 1985 by Hu Yizhou, an aeronautical engineer, who has devoted his entire career and multiple talents to Chinese aviation.

Modernization of industry received the lion's share of attention during the years of 1984 and 1985; however, science and technology, the third modernization, was moving into the limelight.

In May 1984, the State Council approved the first experimental contract system in China's technology research institutes. The organizations chosen for the test program became self-supporting, with no operating expenses supplied by the government, instead signing agreements with both the State and commercial enterprises.[10] The experimental program proved to be so successful that it was adopted nationwide in early 1985.[11]

Feeling that the first three modernizations were becoming well behaved, Deng turned more attention to reforming the PLA, last bastion of the ultra-leftists. In mid-1983 he had begun the delicate reforms, and in March 1985 the announcement that 80,000 veteran officers would retire was evidence that his bold campaign was succeeding.

Assuming continued progress in the ideological battle, recognizing and implementing the talents of intellectuals, emphasis on science and technology, and the acceptance of market techniques of incentives and rewards—whatever it is called—China has the resources to achieve its goals.

---

[10] *China Daily,* May 23, 1985 and *Boeing News,* July 18, 1985.
[11] *China Daily,* May 25, 1984 and March 4, 1985.

Traditionally an energy-poor nation, China has tremendous undeveloped energy sources. According to Li Peng, First Vice-Minister of Water Resources and Electric Power, China's water power resources total 680,000 megawatts in capactiy, 380,000 of which can be tapped, ranking the country's potential hydroelectric power as first in the world.[12] "But the total generating capacity of the large and medium-sized hydroelectric power stations now in operation and the 27 new projects under construction is about 35,000 megawatts, less than one-tenth of the available water power in the country," Li said.

Although China has announced that it will first develop hydroelectric power as far as possible and then build a number of thermal power stations near the coal mines, due attention will be paid to developing nuclear power. The first 1,800-megawatt unit has been assigned to Dayawan, Guangdong Province, close to Hong Kong, for which intensive preparations were already underway in mid-1983. A second 1,800-megawatt nuclear power plant, consisting of two 900-megawatt units of the pressurized water type, will be built in east China to meet the needs of the growing economic development in Shanghai and neighboring provinces, according to Li Peng. He said China also plans to build a third nuclear station in northeast China, a heavy industry base where power has been in short supply.

At the American Nuclear Society's Second Nuclear Technology Exhibit in Beijing in May 1984, it was revealed that current estimates for Chinese nuclear capacity range from 10,000 to 15,000 megawatts under construction and in operation by the year 2000.[13]

To emphasize China's current paucity of total energy on

---

[12] *Ibid.*, June 21, 1983.

[13] *Nuclear News*, July 1984; *China Daily*, February 26, 1985.

tap, it was estimated that approximately 65,000 megawatts are being generated from all sources. This compares with the United States, with installed capacity over 600,000 megawatts, representing a real difference of an order of magnitude and 40 to 1 difference on a per capita basis.[14]

Rich in coal reserves, with at least 55 billion tons, China has assigned priority expansion to eight projects, which after completion will double their total capacity. The eight projects, which together would be capable of an annual production of 100 million tons, are planned to be completed by 1988. These eight projects account for 41 percent of China's current coal output, and represent a large increment of the avowed goal of achieving a national total annual output of 1.2 billion tons by the year 2000.

The Occidental program near Datong is the first joint venture in developing China's coal reserves. Most of the output from the Datong mines will be exported to the huge industrial markets of Japan.

After years of waiting, the race for China's oil is on. In May 1982 the newly formed China National Offshore Oil Corporation (CNOOC) released bidding documents for exploration and production rights on an area half the size of Texas, lying offshore on China's continental shelf. ARCO signed the first contract later in 1982 and began drilling in early 1983. Since its founding in February 1982, CNOOC had signed 11 off-shore contracts with six bidding groups consisting of 18 oil companies from eight countries by the end of October 1983. More contracts are expected.

Overall, Chinese geologists conservatively put the nations' offshore oil reserves at 75 billion barrels. Even if the Western experts' lower estimates of 30 to 40 billion barrels, three to

---

[14] *Nuclear News,* July 1984.

four times Alaska's Prudhoe Bay field, prove to be correct, China is destined to become one of the world's oil powers.

Results from wells drilled by the Chinese themselves and by the French and Japanese companies, which began working the Bohai Gulf in the north and the Gulf of Tonkin in the south in 1981, lent early credence to the industry's optimism.

Initial successes were followed by a series of dry holes in the main drilling zones of the South China Sea, where only one marginal field was discovered after 23 wells had been drilled. In the meantime, large new discoveries added to China's on-shore potential during 1984.[15]

With most experts retaining a high level of confidence that the offshore exploration will eventually yield large quantities of crude oil, China launched a second round of bidding on 93,000 square kilometers of offshore property in early 1985.[16]

Railroads are also receiving priority in the Sixth Five-Year Plan (1981–1985). Of the 70 construction projects approved, 9 are railway projects. Construction is a key to handling the coal shipments for the new production to come on the line.

Water diversion projects, both for flood control and irrigation, are likewise high on the priority list. In May 1983 the PLA engineering corps completed a 11.4-kilometer tunnel through the Yanshan Mountains, a key link in the Tianjin water diversion project, which was brought on the line in the fall of 1983. The canal is bringing 2 billion gallons of water a year from the Luanhe River in northern Hebei Province to Tianjin, the major industrial and port city of northern China. Nearly 300,000 soldiers spent fifteen months cutting the tunnel. The Chinese use units of its huge 4.2-million-man army for many

---

[15]*The Asian Wall Street Journal,* May 24, 1984; *China Daily,* September 22, 1984.
[16]*China Daily,* January 31, 1985.

tasks in flood control, irrigation, and other engineering and construction projects.

After badly underestimating the complexity, cost, and construction time for the Baoshan Iron and Steel plant near Shanghai, the Chinese have now developed a realistic schedule. This project is a prime example of the Chinese willingness to adjust completion dates along with a rationalization of why the planned date was missed, with no apparent embarrassment.

The telephone system is a major impediment to progress, and has recently received a high priority for upgrading. In 1983 China had an average of less than one phone for each 200 people, compared to 114 phones for 200 people in the United States. China's cities, above the county level, had 3.2 telephones per 200 people, and provincial capitals had 4.4, only one-sixth of the world average. In mid-1983 China negotiated a $500-million system of telephones, which will add 700,000 circuits to the 1 million already in place. China has even talked about launching its own communication satellite by 1990.

A major roadblock could be the problem of transfer of sensitive technology. However, even there, progress suddenly appeared imminent, when in the spring of 1983 the United States agreed to move China from the "P" to the "V" category for export controls. The "V" category includes America's NATO allies and non-aligned trading partners such as India and Yugoslavia. Finally in July 1985, President Reagan of the United States and President Li Xiannian of China, signed an agreement for nuclear energy cooperation.

Supporting the new relaxation in export policies on high technology items, former President Richard Nixon called for further enhancement of relations between the two countries in the future, treating China the same as other friendly non-aligned nations. "It's time to remove United States agencies from the straitjacket which requires them to treat China like an adversary," he said.[17]

Labels are hard to remove. Myths die hard. We are caught in a rootedness of familiarity, reluctant to embrace change, and often unable to force it. With the Chinese colossus visibly shifting its weight from the leftist foot to one of moderate policies, and a willingness to bridle the growth of one-fourth of the world's population, it deserves the support of the Western nations. Indeed it may easily be China that influences the Soviet Union to soften its rigid controls, after comparing its own economic miseries with the new Chinese successes.

Having observed the Chinese on a day-to-day, person-to-person basis during the crucial years of 1980–1985, I find it clear that 1979 heralded a landmark change. China will look back but will never turn back.

Three generations of a one child per family reality would result in approximately 850 million Chinese by the year 2050, not only a comfortably supportable number, but a force that could establish China as an economic giant during the next century.

The Special Economic Zones were a harbinger of the potential economic growth. Shenzhen, largest of the four zones, was showing the way. Since 1980, when the zone was established, four major changes have taken place:

Shenzhen grew from a small, sleepy town to a thriving city, where now 19 high-rise buildings of 18 stories or more have sprung up, and 45 additional are under construction; foreign investment and technology has resulted in nearly 700 agreements with foreign firms, totalling U.S. $1.8 billion by March 1984; overall industrial output grew to 720 million yuan in 1983, a 16-fold multiple from 1978; and, finally, the dramatic

---

[17] National Council for U.S.-China Trade, June 1983.

improvement in people's livelihood, boasting a per capita income of 1,571 yuan for industrial workers and 840 yuan for peasants.

By the year 2050, most of the people living in China today would have passed on, the scouring cycle would have produced a new population mix vastly different, with a large technologically trained core and a highly literate mainstream with skills in manufacturing, commercial service, transportation, communication, and computer technology—indeed sharply competitive in the world marketplace, offering modern goods and services.

A massive shift would have taken place from the farms and fields to industry and commerce—machines replacing hands as the farms grew larger. The trend was already apparent as early as mid-1983.[18] It is estimated that by the year 2000, some one-third of the total current rural population will have moved from the farms into industry, bringing with them the new skills that the expanded educational system is expected to provide.[19]

The naysayers have taken a short view of history. They focused too strongly on the waves and failed to notice the ocean.

China, under the new leadership, is willing and ready to follow the economic advice of Deng Xiaoping, who observed "that it does not matter whether a cat is black or white, just so it catches mice."

[18] *China Daily,* September 1, 1983.
[19] *Ibid.,* June 4, 1985.